HOW TO BE AN ESTATE AGENT

Also by Alan Bailey and published by Mercury Books

How To Be A Property Developer

Alan Bailey's

HOW TO BE AN ESTATE AGENT

– and how to get the best out of them!

MERCURY

Published 1991 by Mercury Books
Gold Arrow Publications Ltd
862 Garratt Lane, London SW17 0NB

Set in Plantin & Helvetica by Phoenix Photosetting
Printed and bound in Great Britain by
Mackays of Chatham PLC, Chatham, Kent

British Library in Cataloguing in Publication Data
Bailey, Alan
How to be an estate agent: and how to get
the best out of them!
I. Title
333.330941

ISBN 1–85251–026–9

FOREWORD

When Alan Bailey first asked me to write the foreword to this book, he sent me a copy of his *How to be a Property Developer*, originally published in May 1988, followed by a revised edition last year and soon to be a paperback. That book, he said, had been written not as a textbook but as an entertainment. *How to be an Estate Agent* falls unquestionably into the same category – but, like . . . *Property Developer*, . . . *Estate Agent* has that underlying seriousness which comes from long experience and a mind which knows what has to be done to improve the system and the service which estate agents give.

Estate agents are not popular people. They rank, as the book says, at or near the bottom of the ratings, changing places from time to time with politicians, investigative journalists and double-glazing salesmen. And yet about 66 per cent of householders in this country are now in the class known as owner-occupiers. The figure is rising and will probably reach 75 per cent by the end of the century, if not sooner – give or take a downturn or two. A survey in May 1991 showed that 84 per cent of those interviewed were, or wanted to be, owner-occupiers. These are the buyers and sellers of houses and flats and most of them, whether they like it or not, will buy or sell their homes through an estate agent. All of them will suffer the frustrations and the pitfalls of the house transfer system. All of them will probably use solicitors or a conveyancing firm. Unless they are filthy rich, they will use banks and building societies to fund most of the purchase. Some of them will use builders – and all of them will come up against the national and local authorities in one manifestation or another.

Despite its title, this book has a place on every bookshelf. It has lessons not only for estate agents – although they will enjoy learning from it – but also for buyers, sellers, lenders, lawyers and all those who play a part in the property transfer system. The book veers from history to the crystal ball, from serious commentary to farce, from the theory of carefully considered systems to the reality of day-to-day disasters.

Occasionally, at dinner or cocktail parties or those receptions when only the host knows everybody, I am asked what I do for a living. When I mention the National Association of Estate Agents, everyone seems to take at least a mental pace backwards. The British (unlike the French) are basically polite and will not always say precisely what they think. But it is not difficult to sense the mistrust – and, in some people, even a hint of revulsion. The basic problem is the fact that estate agents have this rotten image; the brush that tars one actually tars the lot. They are the butt of stand-up comics, the natural prey of *Private Eye* and the subject of *Which?* reports which never, somehow, seem to be favourable. It was with some relief, in the heyday of Monty Python, that I noticed that John Cleese had begun to pick on chartered accountants. But it didn't last; eventually, he picked on estate agents too.

Property transfer is a serious business. The purchase of a house or flat is likely to be the biggest financial transaction in a person's lifetime. It should therefore be taken seriously. But anyone who has been at the centre of things knows that there is also humour in abundance and this book overturns every stone to find it. The system of property transfer is extravagant in its complexity. Add the human dimension and you have the ingredients of farce.

Anyone who is an estate agent will have experienced much of what is expressed in this book. Anyone who has bought or sold a house will recognise the frustrations. Those earnest professions who have their place in the order or disorder of things will see themselves as others see them. There are a hundred lessons to be learned because, behind all the humour, this is the reality.

TONY CLARK
Secretary, National Association of Estate Agents

ACKNOWLEDGEMENTS

Authors write acknowledgements at the beginning of their books, usually in a vain attempt to shift the blame on to a string of helpers or the writers of other books to which they have referred when inspiration lapsed.

I take all of the blame for all of this book. It comes from a few tedious years as an estate agent, a few nasty experiences as a seller of houses through estate agents and a few nastier ones as a buyer through an entirely different group of estate agents. It comes from harrowing negotiations with building societies and other funding sources. It comes from arranging insurance cover for bricks and mortar, tiles and timber and, inevitably, contents which are, on the face of it, worthless. It comes from my being an almost impartial observer of the estate agency scene over very many years – and from my knowing far more estate agents, house sellers and house buyers than is good for anyone with a tendency towards neurosis.

There are two people to whom I am particularly grateful. Both are or were estate agents. Both are authors, too. The first is Julian Vivian, who ran Howards of Howardsgate in Welwyn Garden City, until his firm was bought by Connells. His most recently written book is, I think, *Byres and Cellars* – which is the kind of joke you make if you spend too long in the business. The second is Nigel Stephens, once of Whiteheads and who later became a member of the big league. Nigel became the guru of the estate agency world when he wrote a serious textbook *The Practice of Estate Agency*, recommended reading for estate agents both budding and in full bloom. I read both books before I started this one. I didn't refer to them again except to check the spelling of *caveat emptor*. I thank them for the benefit of their wisdom which, they will be glad to know, I have almost totally ignored.

And then there are the literally hundreds of estate agents whom I know as friends and who have provided me with tales of triumph and disaster, some of which I actually believed and used as material for this book, with or without that poetic licence which moves humour into farce. There are also those hundreds of buyers and sellers – the latter including the housebuilders – who have swamped me with strings of complaints about estate agents and their methods, all of which I actually believed because I was the subject of the same kind of complaints.

I also have to thank the professional critics of the estate agency business: the government, the local authorities, the magazine *Which?*, *Private Eye*, Les Dawson and all those other stand-up comedians who poke fun or malice at house agency in particular. They have all done a great deal for the business.

Despite my having been an estate agent, I still have a few friends – and they have to bear with me while books are being written. I thank them all for doing so; and, of course, I thank Maria Munoz, who suffered the monotony of fifty hours of tapes at the last possible moment.

ALAN BAILEY
Belgravia, 1991

CONTENTS

INTRODUCTION

Estate agents have an unenviable reputation. They lurk near
the foot of the popularity ratings, jostling for position with
double-glazing salesmen, politicians, investigative journalists
and similarly untrustworthy professions, callings or common
or garden trades. Few people – other than the house agents
themselves, of course – believe that they actually earn the fees
they charge on the sale of a property. Few people, whether
buyers or sellers, express total – indeed, any – satisfaction at
all with the service they have received at estate agents' hands.
  But estate agents have been with us for a long time. Alternative systems of buying and selling houses have been tried,
tested and largely found wanting in one way or another. At the
end of the day, estate agents actually sell houses and flats and,
even if they don't actually *sell* them, they are usually the
medium of sale simply because they happen to be there.
Buyers and sellers will grumble and mutter. They might
complain to the Office of Fair Trading or even to Esther
Rantzen. In the main, they will sell or buy through an estate
agent, as has been said, simply because he or she is there. The
house agent provides a shop in which pictures and descriptions of the product – houses, bungalows or flats – can be
displayed. The estate agent provides a postal or telephonic
delivery service of information about what is available. The
estate agent keeps a register of hopeful buyers bent on

wrapping the mortgage millstones round their necks. With buyers and sellers beating paths to the estate agent's door, it all looks extraordinarily easy. If money was ever actually paid for old rope, this, on the face of it, is where it went: to the estate agent.

But ask the estate agent what he or she feels about it. He or she works long, often unsocial, hours. He or she – no, we can't keep saying that so, at the risk of offending the ladies, it will be 'he' in future – has to be nice to nearly everybody, from buyer through seller to mortgage manager and a dozen others who get involved in our extraordinary system of property transfer. He has to introduce selection systems so that those who want to buy are given a bundle of particulars nearly relevant to their needs. He believes that every last penny is earned by the sweat of the brow and a small fortune in tranquillisers.

In truth, estate agency is not an easy business. Those who practise it usually work under extraordinary pressures over extended periods. If the market is good, the estate agent works hard by popular demand for his services. If it is bad, the estate agent works even harder because, if he doesn't, he goes out of business. Those he deals with are usually in a highly nervous state. The sellers will want to be sure of selling at just the right time at just the right price to someone who will actually complete the purchase with all the strength of the building societies or other funding sources around him. The buyer will want to buy the same property that everybody else wants, without being outbid, from a seller who won't, at the last moment, throw his hands in the air and decide to stay put for the next ten years.

Estate agency, from whichever standpoint you view it, is surrounded by tension, doubt and incipient anxiety. All participants in the house transfer game have all of those things in varying degrees of intensity – except, perhaps, the lawyers. They stroll unhurriedly through the process with that air of irritating calm which drives everyone else to distraction.

In recent years, a change has occurred in the estate agency business, which has been both dramatic and traumatic. The big battalions, in the form of banks, building societies and other financial houses, have become players in the game, buying up long and not-so-long established house agency firms in order to create, by British standards anyway, gigantic chains of agency outlets. There is good reason: estate agency outlets are often in a prime high street pitch. Estate agents, by their nature, offer open doors to anyone wanting to buy or sell – and those wanting to buy or sell are also targets for a dazzling range of financial services from money lending to insurance. They need money for the house they want to buy, for the furnishings to put inside it . . . they may even want to borrow for the rose garden or the vegetable patch. They are vulnerable to the blandishments of those with money – largely because they are confused, uncertain and so brimful of doubts about everything that they will believe almost anything uttered by anyone in a dark suit and a collar and tie sitting behind a big desk. They have been known to believe those double-glazing salesmen, even before they have moved in.

This book is about all that confusion and it seeks to remove it. Although the house transfer system in this country is a jungle of laws, procedures and unexpected levies for this and that, there is a pathway through it. It is laced with pits, traps and snares for the unwary. It is frequented by fearsome creatures like structural surveyors, whose words of professional wisdom kill more house sales than anything else yet conceived. It is full of time warps – which means that some contributors to the process, like local authority land charges departments, go at a pace quite different from everyone else.

The house transfer system is also full of mysteries and laws of unnatural human behaviour. The mysteries are legion (we will unravel them, of course) and unnatural behaviour by agents, buyers, sellers and everybody else involved is endemic. Some of the combatants – because that is often what they are – speak in languages which the others do not understand. In their worst moments, estate agents write in a shorthand that would have defeated even the combined skills of both Sir Isaac Pitman and Mr Dutton. Estate agents also possess uncanny abilities: the most expensive and efficient cameras and film in their hands take photographs of houses surrounded only by perpetual mists, or which appear to be painted black all over.

But, here in the United Kingdom, we live in a property owning democracy. A surprisingly high proportion of the population has jumped the series of hurdles which the system has erected between tenancy and owner occupation. We are heading fast towards a position in which most of us will be owners. Only a few of us, footloose, fancy free or just plain dropouts, will shy away from the awful responsibilities of the freeholder and the mortgagor.

Those of us who run the course don't do it very often. Some of us do it once, some twice, some even three times. For those who do it more than once, there is usually a gap of at least seven years or so before we do it again. Seven years is a long time, long enough to cloud the memory, ease the heartache and forget the frustrations. So, when we buy or sell and subject ourselves to the system yet again, we are as novices – lambs, as some would have it, to the slaughter.

There are some people who claim to move house every two years. These are not usually home owners; these are soldiers, policemen, diplomats and the like who are liable to be trans-ferred here and there at the drop of a bureaucratic pencil. All they have to do is to crate everything up and move off to the next posting, to a home provided by a benign and benevolent employer who can't stand the thought of anyone in service settling down for a sensible length of time. If there really are home owners who move every two years, they are likely to be dangerous masochists and not at all the kind of people with whom to consort.

So let us enter the extraordinary world of the house transfer system and the people who frequent it. Those people are, you might think, just like you and me. They are, of course – and even estate agents are human beings. They go to school, grow up, marry, have children, own dogs and cars, worry about their tax returns and their bills and even watch bits of *EastEnders*. But, ordinary, everyday folk that we are, when we are subjected to the system, we change; we lose our humanity; we develop that bundle of neuroses which turns love into hate and neighbourliness into open war.

Let us get at it – but slowly.

1 HISTORY AND OTHER BUNK

It is difficult to judge how it all started. Until relatively recently, home ownership was not widespread. In the old days there were, on the one hand, the landowners and, on the other, the tenantry. People either paid a rent for their home or worked hard for it by the sweat of the brow or the callousing of the hands. Landowners, who included the filthy rich, the Church and the Crown, had chaps called factors, land agents or bailiffs who managed their estates. Management took in the occasional repair and infrequent maintenance of the cottages or other accommodation provided for gamekeepers, farmhands, odd-jobmen and all the other skills necessary to sustain the great estates and the quality of life their owners enjoyed.

Villages or hamlets grew up around the great houses and relied on them for their economic well-being. The landowners owned nearly everything. Most of them had, of course, been given it in the first place as an award for knightly service to the sovereign. Some people, like Nell Gwyn, were given land and buildings for nightly service to the sovereign, and her heirs still own slabs of real estate which provide a generous income from the rents their tenants pay.

Not everyone was in the service of the great houses, well, not directly anyway. Some wanted to build their own accommodation which offered mixed uses: shopkeepers, black-smiths, innkeepers and other entrepreneurial spirits who valued their independence. They still faced the problem that the land on which they wanted to build was owned by some drunken baron. So they took leases – some short, some long–recognising that, sooner or later, depending on the length of the lease, the land and what they had put on it would revert to the drunken baron or his equally drunken offspring.

As industry emerged, mill and other owners adopted the same paternalistic approach for sound, selfish reasons. Houses were clustered around mills and collieries, paid for by the owner and rented to his workers. He, of course, lived up at t'manor, beyond sniffing distance of his workers whose houses sported only a chilly outside loo and a tin bath in front of the fire on Friday nights.

Landlords, whether baronial or industrial, were occasionally short of cash. Then, they were prepared to sell land freehold. Ownership by the common man (although he would not usually wish to describe himself as such) began to be established. Even so, the country was not mobile by modern standards and the transfer of freehold ownership was not frequent enough to provide an adequate base for an estate agency business. But the beginnings were being formed: there were the factors and land agents. They were still at the centre of things, where they could be the intermediaries for the transfer of farms, houses and hovels. It is in the nature of humanity to seek payment for any kind of intermediary activity – and the medieval intermediaries could be as avaricious as Shylock, for less reason.

While the framework for modern agency was being established, other things were happening which were to have a profound effect on agency's ultimate success. There was the Industrial Revolution: underpaid farmhands poured into the urban areas to make their fortunes. The birthrate began to gallop and the growing population demanded more accommodation which, in the main, the old style industrial landlords usually provided.

Ownership, whether freehold, leasehold, or simple possession through tenancy, brought its own kind of responsibility. Houses, even the most humble, had to be furnished. All manner of trades and near-professions developed to slake the thirst for possessions: upholsterers, carpenters and other trades directly related to property ownership or possession began to take on incidental activity. They knew about buildings; they knocked about the area and knew that Mrs Heppelthwaite wanted to move. It wasn't difficult to become an intermediary and to take whatever payment was offered or demanded for the service.

In fact, some of those who know about these things regard auctioneering as the roots of estate agency. Some of the rest regard surveying as the true parent. And the remainder come down strongly in favour of the lawyer. It is, therefore, difficult to know at whose door to lay the blame for the present state of affairs.

The lawyers must certainly take a large share of the responsibility. They knew all about their clients' property. They knew all about their clients' financial needs. And, of course, they prepared the conveyances by which property was transferred. At least, they made the decisions about the drafting of

conveyances. The documents themselves were written out (or engrossed) by scriveners. These were clerks who could actually wield a quill to good effect and who could spell – well, almost. If they couldn't actually spell a word, they had a serious crack at interpreting the phonetics, sometimes with a delightful inconsistency which makes reading old deeds almost as entertaining as the average TV panel game.

What the scriveners did, of course, was to absorb knowledge about what we now pompously call the residential property market. They became expert conveyancing lawyers themselves but, more importantly, they became a kind of property Mafia. By the late 1600s, the scriveners were preparing the equivalent of our present agency lists of properties for sale on the one hand and budding buyers on the other. The properties they dealt with were relatively up-market – landed estates, farms and town houses for the rich – because most of the lower orders still lived in rented accommodation or curled up to sleep in doorways which, they say, nearly a million impoverished souls still do in this 'loadsamoney' country of ours.

Another 'profession' which began to dip its fingers into the tasty pie of real estate was that of undertaker. When the master of a house died, it was the undertaker who

'undertook' the arrangements for the disposal of his mortal remains. It was a short, and often neatly executed, step to 'undertake' all the other arrangements. Disposal of the family home and its contents seemed not far removed from the rest of the undertaker's services. A few long established firms of enormous respectability can trace an undertaker among their forebears. These days, what is known as 'coffin following' is not regarded as a savoury professional practice, although the modern estate agent is not averse to a careful scrutiny of the 'births, deaths and marriages' columns of the press as a marketing aid.

The surveyors (the word comes from the French word *surveilleur* which means manager or overseer) looked after estates. When you look after a sizeable estate, it is a good idea to know what you are supposed to be looking after. So the surveyors took to preparing plans of the areas under their management. As the motto of the Royal Institution of Chartered Surveyors says, 'there is measure in all things' (or something like that) and soon the surveyors were looked upon as experts in the measurement of value. All this drawing of plans and valuation skill placed them in a good position for their ultimate onslaught on the property market. However, in the sixteenth and seventeenth centuries, they tended to be subservient to the lawyers and the auctioneers.

It would not be unfair to describe the auctioneers as a fairly motley lot. They came from all manner of trades: literally butchers, bakers and candlestick makers. Auctions started with goods and chattels. A butcher might decide to auction his meat, particularly if it had been hanging about for a while without the benefit of a cold store. Wine merchants certainly used the auction system to dispose of imported or smuggled stocks.

Life was rather more leisurely in those days and the auctioneers had to shake the bidding populace from their customary torpor. They sold 'by the candle' or 'by the sandglass'. A candle was lit and, as it spluttered down to an agreed mark, that was the time allowed for the bidding for a certain lot. The sandglass was the equivalent of the egg-timer (before it went electronic) and was used to the same purpose. But more of this later.

The auctions were advertised by poster and word of mouth and those with goods to sell might ask the auctioneer, be he butcher or wine merchant, to include them in his auction sale. The butcher might, therefore, find himself selling furniture, farm stock, bric-a-brac and a few cabbages. Farmers auctioned livestock and, in the same way, added to their lots with all kinds of extras. It wasn't long before land and buildings came under the gavel. But these had higher values. The auctioneer, of course, took a commission and he (and the landowner) had to be sure that the price was right. This brought the overseers – the surveyors – back into the game in their role as valuers and the producers of plans so that the auctioneer knew what he was selling and the successful bidder knew what he was buying. And then the lawyers had to do the conveyancing bit, adding to their knowledge of the property market.

Soon, everybody was at it: the auctioneers themselves from a wide diversity of trades and occupations, the lawyers and the surveyors. So big a business did auctioneering become that it attracted the attention of government. Just as today, if something becomes too successful, the government taxes it, an excise duty was placed on auction proceeds and the auctioneers themselves had to pay an annual licence fee.

What was happening, of course, was that a body of expertise was being created. In this country, as in many others which are sophisticated enough to know a good thing when they see it, expertise is jealously guarded. In 1799, the Select Society of Auctioneers was created in London. It was probably the first closed shop in the property business.

You may have heard the phrase 'the learned babble'. It was Carlyle who coined it: he called it 'the learned babble of the saleroom and varnishing auctioneer'. Those of us who acquired our sparse knowledge of periods and styles through occasional, and sometimes urgent, scrutiny of the *Encyclopaedia of Architecture* and the *Dictionary of Antiques* crawl from auction rooms feeling every inch the Philistine (some of whom, you will remember, were fairly tall). The erudition, the easy familiarity with priceless treasures or properties we cannot afford, the casual reference to some historic fact or anecdote about the artist, architect or craftsman – those are the things which cut the layman down to size.

Certainly, some extraordinary characters have risen from the ranks of auctioneers of real and personal property. Certainly, it is no profession for the shy, the modest and the unassuming. The average struggle along – expert in the valuation of the lots they offer, undoubtedly, but without any obvious flair, without panache. The best are born with a skill which tempts bids, which paints word pictures beyond value and which confers an unerring capacity to drop the hammer at precisely the right moment. But only the very best justify the definition, given by Ambrose Bierce in *The Devil's Dictionary*, of an auctioneer as a man who proclaims with a hammer that he has picked a pocket with his tongue.

Auctioneering is, they say, as old as man himself. Its history is absorbing stuff and the variations over the centuries capture the imagination. Writing in *The Estate Agent*, Michael Newman of W.H.Lane & Son referred to 'auction at the candle'. Prize ships were usually sold in this way. A candle was marked with a line and lit; bids were then accepted and the sale was completed at the last bid before the candle finally burnt the mark away. One imagines that the start of such an auction was

slow and finished with a flurry of bids and, no doubt, considerable disagreement arose as to when the mark actually disappeared! 'Sale by sand' was a variation on this theme, the sand trickling through an hour glass replacing the candle. It was certainly a more definite period of time, and one not affected by draughts!

Of all the personalities who ranged the auction rooms of this country, and the London Auction Mart in particular, one stands out. He is regarded as the father of estate agency English, the sire of acceptable hyperbole, the master of flamboyant description. He would have sent the Office of Fair Trading rushing hotfoot for their reference books, and the Advertising Standards Authority for their sal volatile. But they need not have been concerned: he was never accused of unfair practice. There is no record of a bidder objecting to an unnecessary or misleading adjective. He was the man with a golden tongue.

He was George Henry Robins. George Robins was sired by an auctioneer. His father, Henry, one of the founders of the Society of Auctioneers in 1799, came to London from Gloucestershire in 1775. He acquired the auctioneers' practice carried on by Abraham Langford in the north-east corner of the Piazza in Covent Garden. Langford had died in 1774 at the age of 63. He was a man of distinguished ability as an auctioneer and playwright and had himself succeeded a well-known practitioner, Christopher Cock – 'Auctioneer Cock', as he was dubbed in 1748.

George Robins was born in May 1777. His first appearance on the rostrum was some time before he was nineteen when, unexpectedly, owing to his father's illness, he was called upon to take the latter's place at a sale in Yorkshire. He handled the auction successfully. 'Could he but then', wrote Mr Grant, the author of a short biographical sketch of George Robins, 'have looked through the long history of time and there have seen the lovely estates of England, Scotland, Ireland and Wales which were destined to fall in after years before his hammer!'

The same writer described the style and the dress of the man who during the next fifty years rose to a position in the profession which is unlikely ever to be surpassed:

Mr George Robins displayed the most consummate tact, from the moment he mounted the rostrum until he again descended from it. Before he regularly introduced to the notice of his audience the property about to be disposed of, he was sure to make some kindly familiar observation to them, which was calculated to put them on good terms with him and themselves. As the Auction Mart was small, there was usually a number of persons about the doors when he entered. In that case Mr Robins, in a good-natured, characteristic way, would say, if the weather were hot: 'do come inside my good friends, you'll be much cooler inside.' If the weather were cold, he would accost them with: 'do, my good friends, come a little farther in; you'll be much warmer if you do.' If the weather were neither hot nor cold, but in that medium state which is so agreeable to the constitution, then the prince of auctioneers would thus apostrophise the company: 'do, gentlemen, come inside, you'll be much more comfortable than in lounging about the door: besides, my friends, I always like to see my auditors.' In short, in all seasons, during all weathers and in all circumstances, Mr Robins had something in the shape of conciliatory phraseology for his auditors the moment he entered the Auction Mart and before he even uttered a word respecting the property about to be sold.

This being done, he would put himself into an erect position, carefully adjusting with both hands the little hair which latterly still surmounted the crown of his head. He would then enter heart and soul with astonishing earnestness into the business of the day. And, oh! the rare ability with which he executed the task he had undertaken! How he would eulogise the taste and judgement of his hearers. How he would coax, as it were, 'offer after offer' from them! Who shall even attempt to do justice to the richness and ingenuity of his eulogiums on the qualities of the properties entrusted to him? Shakespeare, we are told, first exhausted worlds and then imagined new. Leave out the 'l' in the term 'worlds', and the same may be said with perfect truth of Mr George Robins, when professionally engaged at the Auction Mart. He did exhaust words and then, with an ability peculiarly his own, imagined and applied new ones in the prodigality of his encomiums on the excellence of the property consigned to his care. He was, in point of fact, a Shakespeare in his own peculiar way. What Avon's immortal bard was in the eye of the ideal world, he was in the material world!

Here was a consummate actor. During his career, George Robins was a man with many interests in literary and dramatic circles. His friends included Byron, Sheridan, Theodore Hook and John Kemble. He and Sheridan – no doubt with others – dined one evening at the Tavistock Hotel with 'the first gentleman of Europe', at the latter's particular request, when His Majesty is said to have been vastly entertained. To other princes of the blood, George Robins is reported to have been a most complaisant banker. He was for years an active director of Drury Lane Theatre and later of Covent Garden Theatre. His first wife had borne him no children, but in 1832 he took as his second wife a Miss Losack, a young lady of considerable beauty but with a less considerable talent as an actress; she bore him seven children. Prior to his second marriage, during the lifetime of his first wife, another resident in George Robin's household was Mrs Robin's niece. She was Miss Isabella Mackinlay, who later married one of George Robin's nephews. During her residence with her aunt and uncle, she often burned midnight oil looking up references and quotations with which to embellish her uncle's rostrum appearances. He is said to have lived at the rate of £12,000 a year – which, before 1847 when he died, was no mean income, and he managed to leave an estate of £140,000.

But the material evidence of success is nothing compared with the man's language. His preparation was careful. He was well supported by his researchers, including young Isabella Mackinlay, his wife, his children, and his faithful assistant, Roper, who was always at hand. His best preparatory work is said to have been done in the pavilion in his garden with a glass of brandy and water at his elbow. He affected flamboyant humility. He usually adopted one of two methods for his preamble. He began by expressing the 'profound dismay of the humble individual called upon to describe so lovely a property to perform properly his fearsome task' or – if pressed for time – he would begin: 'It would too closely partake of works of supererogation for the individual . . . (etc.) to attempt to portray so delectable a spot'. He would then perhaps add a long quotation from a guidebook or other writing rescued from oblivion by his niece.

Take, as an example, this extract from his description of the Piercefield Estate sold in June 1833. It is said to be one of his best efforts and includes the following description of the River Rye:

The Golden Wye

. . . whose waters shine with brilliancy that well becomes its name. The enlivening freshness which pervades all around – the meandering of the rapid stream below, whose murmuring sound falls upon the ear – the opposite amphitheatre of Cliffs – the perforated Banegar Rocks, beautifully studded with yew trees, and with Wyndcliff in its termination, all towering one above the other; contrasted with the peace and quietude of the luxuriant vale below, forms such a picture that even favoured England's clime cannot find a compeer so grand, so noble and at the same time so lovely. In this little Paradaisical spot, an uneven walk leads to the Cold Bath, situate in a most refreshing spot; midway on the precipice (at this point less steep) a path winds down to new Elysian Fields – it is here that the fearful precipice bursts upon the view with all its terrific grandeur, whilst the huge fragments of Ivy-crowned rocks rise from among the underwood and present themselves with all their pristine native rudeness. The sublimity here imparted, the never-ending variety, the Panorama which is beheld from the Wyndcliff, the gigantic efforts of Nature and the pictorial effect must be seen to form a moderate conception of its grandeur; and the delight which is experienced on reaching the top of the Wyndcliff, well repays the occasional repine that is indistinctly heard whilst labouring up the steep of this tremendous mountain.

And how about this? – about the famed Castle of Devizes, sold in 1843:

Historical associations of surpassing interest connected with the property are too many to be enumerated in this brief sketch; a few only will be appended to this short analysis. It is not intended to hammer up the feelings of the reader by dwelling on the horrors of the fearful dungeons and the state prison, or refer to the cruelty and bad taste of those degenerate times, but rest content by alluding especially to the interesting facts, that the Castle of Devizes, erected by Roger, Bishop of Salisbury, in the reign of King Henry I, was for centuries honoured by being selected by the Monarchs of England as the Dowry and Palace of the Queens.

And he goes on later:

Nature and art have lavished their richest stores on the beautiful pleasure grounds surrounding the castle. They are singly diversified in form and delightfully adorned with ornamental trees, shrubs and flowers. The interminable winding walks which are ever developing a varied succession of charming views, lead to cool retreats or sunny seats where the enviable possessor of what has been ASSIMILATED TO ELYSIUM 'may rule the shade or court the breeze, at will'. From the summit of the Flag Tower a panorama is seen unequalled for extent and richness in England extending over the rich champagne country, until it is lost in the distant parts of England and Wales.

Three years later, he sold Forde Abbey, close to Axminster. The particulars of sale were heavy with quotations and are far too long to reproduce. However, it contains this gem:

> And to omit a panygyric upon THE ANCIENT TAPES-TRY that adorns the State Rooms, would approach sacrilege. It really and truly may be accounted the wonder and admiration of the world. It fearlessly challenges a rival; and the writer is exceedingly desirous that the reader should not for one moment charge this description with being too vivid. He may rest assured here is no flight of fancy, but a veritable and unassuming report.

In the same particulars, he states: 'The tenantry are very respectable, and without One Guinea of Arrear; indeed, the latter word could not find a place in their vocabulary'.

It is difficult to guess what the Consumers' Association would make of all this. Even Mrs Thatcher, before her departure, demanded that estate agents be more honest in their descriptions and her concern had all-party support. There is, however, something bizarre about any politician demanding honesty from anybody else, even estate agents. The descriptions in our contemporary particulars of sale are anaemic by comparison, whatever you may think of them, and it says much for our shifts in style and education. Faced with a panegyric, someone within the saleroom would, these days, want to bid for it.

There is much more of Robins. The extracts given here are taken from the paper presented by his grandson, Piers Robins FAI, on 4 February 1926 and printed in the Auctioneers' and Estate Agents' Institute's Journal of that period. There is a small library of his work and words – bound volumes of his sale particulars – held in the Royal Institution of Chartered Surveyors in Great George Street. Perhaps his most famous sale was the contents of Strawberry Hill, the seat of Horace Walpole. The sale lasted a month and the catalogue ran to 250 pages – page upon page of vivid writing tinged with histrionic pomp and circumstance and awash with quotation.

George Robins made the most of everything. In 1840, speaking in the House of Commons during the debate on the Corn Bill, Sir Robert Peel was driven to say: 'I do hope that Hon. Gentlemen will in future refer to my statements and not to that authority, high though it be, whose lucubrations they may have time to peruse – I mean Mr George Robins, the auctioneer'. To save you the trouble of looking it up, a lucubration is a literary work, especially of pedantic or elaborate character, produced by candlelight. I know exactly how Sir Robert Peel felt.

While George Robins was practising his rhetoric, private ownership of land and buildings was widening. The market was increasing; skills were developing. The separate streams of expertise began to challenge each other for the privilege of monopoly. To this day, the several challenges have not succeeded. Estate agency is not a monopoly. It is not even the sole province of the auctioneers, the surveyors or the lawyers. Any old Tom, Dick or Harriet can call themselves an estate agent or even a property consultant, which in residential terms may sound a little grander, but in reality means just the same.

2 THE ESTABLISHMENT

Men – for reasons of personal insecurity, common interests, self-preservation or means of escape from domestic bliss – like forming themselves into unions, clubs, lodges and societies. Some prefer words like 'institute' or 'institution'. It was always so. As soon as boys are old enough to toddle, their minds turn to the formation of gangs with secret signs and passwords. Women were usually excluded from these gatherings but, in these more enlightened days, they have become full members of most things. They do, of course, have their own clubs, associations and gangs, and even groups within male-dominated associations and institutes, but they have been clever enough to give their own organisations such sexist titles as the 'Mothers' Union', the 'Women's Institute', the 'Business and Professional Women's Guild' and 'Women in Property', which successfully exclude male membership and interference.

This practice of men getting together in gangs is not just a British foible. The trend is international: tongs appeared in China; Al Capone got things organised in Chicago; the Mafia went international in a big way. It is all part of the same syndrome. The emerging professions in this country were no exception. We have already heard about the creation of the Select Society of Auctioneers which was formed in 1799. As the years rolled on, a professional body was formed for every conceivable professional activity – lawyers, accountants, surveyors, land agents and, of course, estate agents.

The nineteenth century saw the creation of what is now the Royal Institution of Chartered Surveyors which, a hundred years later, was to absorb the Chartered Auctioneers' and Estate Agents' Institute and the Chartered Land Agents' Society. A proposal for a merger between the RICS and the Incorporated Society of Valuers and Auctioneers failed at the last hurdle, but no doubt there will be another try in due course. Some time ago, ISVA (initials are used in the property world to add to its mystique) actually sought a Royal Charter of which the RICS took the dimmest of views. The RICS is undoubtedly the leading professional body of the land and sets stringent examinations for entry or makes sure that exempting degrees or diplomas are as good as they should be. For many years of its long life, the RICS looked upon estate agency as being somewhere below the salt, and there is a sneaking suspicion among many of its estate agency members that it still does.

The reason for this is that the RICS is essentially a conglomerate: it has distinct divisions in its structure. There are land and hydrographic surveyors who are responsible for mapping the world and charting the seas and who, not to put too fine a point on it, look upon themselves as the real surveying intellectuals. This is probably true, because they are often the poorest. Then there are quantity surveyors who measure and price the ingredients of buildings in terms of labour and materials. They are a peculiarly British invention, but are highly regarded and looked upon as indispensable by some leaders in the property industry. Property people outside the UK (except where British colonial influence once had sway) are not so sure and some UK developers are also moving towards that view. And then there are agricultural and forestry surveyors – the land agents – who have a considerable station in life because they rub shoulders with the landed gentry. They tend to have freezers stuffed with trout, salmon and birds of varying kinds.

The mining surveyors – not great in number but with a heavy responsibility for safety in mines – are also in the RICS structure. But by far the greatest number of surveyors comes under the broad classification of general practice. This division formerly included all of those who practised estate agency in one form or another. When this came about, there was an immediate revolution and another division was formed – planning and development – to house all those general practice surveyors who didn't want to be linked with estate agency and who practised as investment, planning and other kinds of consultant surveyors without dirtying their hands with estate agency.

In RICS terms, estate agency covers commercial, industrial, retail and residential premises for letting or sale. What is sad, and just a little ironic, is that even the largest commercial surveying practice with a mammoth international reputation relies heavily on agency for its bread and butter and a fair measure of its jam. Highly professional 'rating' departments of professional practices don't normally make gigantic profits unless the government suddenly decides to introduce the uniform business rate, throw in a revaluation and rely on the media to frighten to death every businessman in the country. Management, the traditional overseeing function of the surveyor, doesn't actually make a fortune either. But agency – commercial agency – well, that is a different story. Without agency, a host of valuable professional services would probably be unaffordable. And, of course, agency brings to the practice the streetwise knowledge that supports the professional function of the valuer, the investment surveyor and the development consultant.

The reason for the establishment attitudes was that estate agency, even the toffee-nosed, commercial kind which is inexorably linked with residential agency in the minds of the public, has a rotten image. Nevertheless, many chartered surveyors in general practice who rely on residential estate agency for that bread, butter and jam also act as valuers, investment surveyors and development consultants, although sometimes in a small way. One body which, when it was formed in 1962, was uninhibited about its relationship with estate agency is the National Association of Estate Agents. We will come back to the Association in a moment.

Now it's a funny thing about professional bodies that, although ostensibly created as a kind of élitist closed shop, they immediately fasten on to the device of protection of the public interest. Protection of the public interest demands that only members of the professional body itself should be allowed to serve anybody – for fees, that is. Anybody outside the élitist closed shop is immediately looked upon as an unqualified charlatan whose professional services – if they could possibly be described as professional – would lead to total disaster or financial ruin, if not both. The consequence of this is that some of those who are excluded from the professional club sulk for a year or two and then rush off and form another professional body. The new body struggles, manfully and womanfully, working out codes of professional conduct and issues carefully worded statements about the unqualified charlatans who are outside *their* particular club. The new body adds its voice to the voice of the first professional body and the noise becomes loud enough to persuade some of those still totally unattached to form yet another professional body. The new body sets about writing a code of professional conduct – but there is no point in going on like this because the message must be reasonably clear.

There is usually a reason other than mere petulance which prompts a group of otherwise normal people to form a professional body. There is usually a threat.

Before we examine the threat as it affected estate agency, let us just recapitulate. We have seen that estate agency grew from a hotch-potch of activities which gave their practitioners access to the profitable world of real estate. Those practitioners got there through a mix of awareness and opportunism. What they did, of course, eventually demanded a discipline – a core of knowledge, the drawing together of a mix of law, economics and construction, as well as feet fairly and squarely in the market-place so that they knew what was going on.

Once the practitioners formed their clubs, they codified what others had to know before they could join. Examination of potential entrants in the early years was not necessarily formal. There were no examination papers. There were, in most cases, interviews. There were, of course, nepotism, favouritism and any other '-ism' you care to mention. In fact, it was the old boys' club in its rawest form, the old boy network, exclusive and excluding all but the chosen few.

The world of real estate seemed to proliferate professional societies. So wide was the range of services that the Royal Institution of Chartered Surveyors, the Chartered Auctioneers' and Estate Agents' Institute and the Chartered Land Agents' Society lived happily together without too much conflict. All of these were fairly august bodies who looked down on lesser societies from the lofty perch of 'charter', but the RICS looked down on everybody. They had themselves grown largely through merger and in 1968 the three chartered bodies came together under the title of the Royal Institution of Chartered Surveyors.

Before that happened, there had been several attempts to introduce statutory control of estate agency. The first, in 1888, was withdrawn by its sponsor after strong opposition. The next attempt was made in 1914 and that went the same way. There were further attempts in 1923, 1928 and 1936; they all failed. By 1952, the principal societies which had previously opposed statutory control had changed their minds and supported the Harry Legge-Bourke Bill, but that failed too. The Jones Bill in 1965 had the support of no fewer than ten 'societies of the land' and everyone thought that this would go through. It provided for the setting up of an Estate Agents' Council which would be responsible for ensuring a reasonable standard of competence and a whole range of things which amounted to protection of the public interest. Despite all the optimism, the Bill failed because the Wilson Government resigned and went to the country – although the Estate Agents' Bill was not the primary reason.

The ten societies had, by this time, become fixed on the idea of some kind of control. They created, quite voluntarily, the Estate Agents' Registration Council which came into being in 1967. The leading professional bodies, with their strong educational policies and tough examinations, were sitting side by side with other societies which had no educational policies at all and no examinations worthy of the name. It was not surprising that the leading bodies lost their enthusiasm for the council which offered nothing for their members that they did not already do for themselves. So, it failed too and all the paraphernalia of offices and forms and furniture was broken up. One of the objects of the Estate Agents' Registration Council, as its name indicated, was to register all estate agents and prevent practice by those who were not registered. However wide the holes in the sieve might have been, it was at least a sieve.

One of the results of all this introspection on the part of the professional bodies and their members was that the Government had begun to take an interest in the subject of estate agency. The Government's primary concern was also to protect the public interest. There are two points to make. First, the Government wanted to see the abandonment of anything that smelled of a restrictive practice, including mutually agreed fee scales. Secondly, the Government looked upon estate agency as a commercial activity, not a professional one, and did not seem too concerned to impose high examination standards of entry. This last point suited some of the ten societies but certainly not all of them. The chartered bodies with rigorous examination standards would probably have preferred those standards, or something very near them, to have been applied.

In 1975, the Government issued a consultative document about the regulation of estate agency. Two years and a few dozen reams of paper later, the Government's own proposals were published, but it was left to Mr Bryan Davies MP to introduce the proposals as a Private Member's Bill. The result was the Estate Agents Act of 1979. It has to be said that, by the standards of the informed, the Act did not go far enough. Only bits of it were brought into effect anyway and there seemed – and still seems – to be no determination on the part of Government to introduce those parts of the Act which might begin to have some bite. This attitude reflects the Government's view that estate agency is a commercial activity and that, if it seeks to ban restrictive practices which are against the public interest, then it should not itself impose restrictions on entry to that commercial activity.

So, although we now have a regulatory act, it doesn't actually regulate very much at all. Anyone can still become an estate agent merely by doing the job. He or she doesn't have to know anything about the subject; he or she doesn't have to be a member of this or that professional body. He or she just gets on with it and, if nothing goes wrong, no one will interfere. If someone alleges that something is wrong, the body responsible for determining whether it is wrong or whether it is right is the Office of Fair Trading.

Earlier, we mentioned the National Association of Estate Agents. The latter organisation (and you may have noticed this) is now the only body with the words 'estate agents' in its title. There was at one time a Chartered Auctioneers' and Estate Agents' Institute, but that merged with the Royal Institution of Chartered Surveyors and the Chartered Land Agents' Society. The members of all three societies became chartered surveyors of one kind or another. A very high proportion of the overall membership was in what the business calls 'general practice', which means that many of them were actually residential estate agents. Of course, they were other things as well. Their offices offered valuations, structural surveys, rating advice, planning consultancy and commercial work – a whole range of things which put them a cut above the simple house agent.

The National Association of Estate Agents had no such pretensions. In fact, I am surprised they didn't call themselves the National Association of House Agents. They made no bones about being estate agents. It has to be said that those who created the Association did so to oppose one or other of the Private Members' Bills which would have given unfair precedence to the chartered societies who, on the face of it, were really after a closed shop. It also has to be said that the Association's creators were very bright indeed and, in professional terms, probably as professional as those who regarded themselves as the real professionals. The really clever ploy was to call themselves the National Association of Estate Agents. In consequence, the government looked to that young, upstart association for advice and comment on its proposals on equal terms with the longer-established and heavily respected chartered bodies who called themselves anything but estate agents. There was much fluttering in the dovecotes over that, particularly among the non-estate agency members of the older and very distinguished societies.

The National Association put its muscle – and that all-important name – behind what became the Estate Agents Act of 1979. The association is still relatively small in numbers – somewhere between 9,000 and 10,000 compared with the Royal Institution of Chartered Surveyors' membership of 60,000, nearly half of whom act as or work for firms which practise as estate agents of one kind or another, though not necessarily in the purely residential field.

So we have the Royal Institution of Chartered Surveyors, the Incorporated Society of Valuers and Auctioneers and the National Association of Estate Agents. Each has a code of professional conduct – separately and independently drafted, of course, but remarkably similar. All of them claim with some gusto to be concerned primarily with the public interest – without even a smile on their faces or the hint of a tic. And those three separate societies represent only estate agency. The Law Society represents the lawyers. There is an association for the building societies; if there is a builder involved in your particular transaction anywhere along the line, he could be a member of any one of three or four bodies. And they all issue codes of conduct too with disciplinary procedures to back them up. The establishment is therefore wedded to the principle of public protection.

There remains, of course, the great unwashed – those who are members of no professional or trade body at all. There are many of them who are, to use the favoured word, unattached. Although being unattached gives the impression of freedom to provide the best possible service, it does also bring its little hardships. Those who are members of the big battalions are what is known as 'bonded', that is to say the users of their services are at least partly protected from defections, using clients' money to back the loser in the 3 o'clock at Kempton or just swanning off with the secretary to live in Bali. The unattached have to buy their own bond or insurance, and it can be mightily expensive.

Lording over all these attached and unattached estate agents is the Office of Fair Trading. If any member of the house-buying or house-selling public feels that he has cause for complaint about an estate agent, his complaint can be lodged with the Office of Fair Trading. That office then investigates the complaint and, if it is found to be justified, the Office of Fair Trading can prevent the estate agent from acting as an agent. It can also impose all kinds of dire penalties which actually cost money. This is rather more than most of the professional bodies can do. Their only sanction is really to kick the offender out of the club – although the National Association of Estate Agents can impose a fine not exceeding £1,000 for each breach of the Rules of conduct plus unlimited costs. This does not actually mean that he, the offender, has to stop being an estate agent; but the Office of Fair Trading can ban a proven offender from so acting. We will come back to the letter of the law a little later. This chapter is merely intended to give some preliminary hints of the dog's breakfast which is made of the house transfer business.

There is, however, one law which, as this goes to press, has just received Royal Assent. As it moved from Bill to Act, it suffered a change of name. This is the Property Misdescriptions Act of 1991, which started life as the Estate Agents Property Misdescriptions Bill. Someone then realised that it wasn't only estate agents who sold houses, so the Act now covers everyone. The description or misdescription of property for sale is worthy of closer study.

---

3 DESCRIPTION

We spent some little time on the background of Mr George Henry Robins, the celebrated auctioneer born in the eighteenth century, whose descriptive style was designed to captivate his bidders. This was merely to put into perspective the twentieth century debate on estate agents' description of property, which culminated in the presentation to Parliament of the Estate Agents Property Misdescriptions Bill. The National Association of Estate Agents (yes, it's them again) were quick to point out that lawyers, building societies and any Tom, Dick or Harriet could offer houses for sale – and what about all that commercial stuff which was hanging about with moss on the 'For Sale' boards? The Bill, following these representations, was called the Property Misdescriptions Bill, was enacted with that title and we now have the Property Misdescriptions Act, 1991.

It is one of the ironies of life that politicians, those inveterate strangers to the truth, resent anyone else stretching the facts to meet the circumstances. Estate agents have been the target of the politicians in this respect for so long that they have now shrugged off some of the latest onslaughts on their vocabularies. Estate agents are not the purveyors of elegant prose: they are the purveyors of houses, bungalows and flats which their clients desperately want to sell. Occasionally, they have to make the best of a thoroughly bad job; and, because they make a thoroughly bad job of making the best of it, they fall out with the politicians bent on protecting their electorate's interests.

But what are their electorate's interests? If, as they say, half of their electorate are buyers, the other half are sellers. It is, as often as not, the sellers who insist on florid description, on that hint of hyperbole, on that over-zealous description of a garden plot that would make Adam quail and Eve blush. After all, they, the owners, are as anxious as the estate agent to sell the damned place.

What estate agents know – and, apparently, politicians don't – is that there is no pattern to the minds of the house buyers whether first time, second time or even more. People buy a particular house, bungalow or flat for the most extra-ordinary reasons. There was the case of the stained glass window. The window, or, in fact, dozens of them, had obviously been bought as a job lot by a mid-1930s builder of traditional semis in an East London suburb. They were circu-lar, about two feet across and, artistically, left much to be desired. They portrayed at least one tree, a bit of grass, a hint of sea and some cloudless sky. The builder, who obviously knew more about marketing than most, had introduced into the front parlour (as it was sometimes called in the mid-1930s) one of these wretched windows. A potential buyer, expressing a desire for a two-bedroomed semi somewhere east of Aldgate, was persuaded by a despairing agent to take a look at the place, which had three bedrooms and was above the potential buyer's price range. The potential buyer brought Mrs Potential Buyer and she fell in love with the stained glass window. The estate agent, always anxious to improve his knowledge of the wayward ways of potential buyers, asked why. The sun, she said, was shining through it and it made a pretty pattern on the carpet; which was nothing to write home about anyway and would probably be consigned to the bonfire as soon as the sale was completed.

Mrs Potential Buyer normally makes a bee-line for the kitchen, the master bedroom and the main bathroom if the house is blessed with two. She pours scorn on all of these while Mr Potential Buyer is looking with deep longing at the derelict potting shed to which he imagines he might, at some time, escape for a quiet smoke. The point of all this is that, no matter what the agents might say, no matter how he might describe the building to be sold, his imagination will never encompass everything that will appeal to a potential buyer, whether Mr or Mrs or both. The examples are legion.

Buyers who, they say, set their hearts on a bungalow in Clacton are just as likely to end up with a detached house or even a flat in Frinton. What has taken them to the house or flat in Frinton is, usually, the zeal of the estate agent, zeal built on exasperation, or his description of the property in his detailed particulars of sale. In the case of the wretched stained-glass window, the estate agent hadn't even mentioned it in his particulars. Quite apart from the fact that it was a standard fitting to all of the houses on the estate, the agent swallowed hard when he saw it, because he was a sensitive man and liked opera. His personal tastes did not extend to poorly designed stained-glass windows in suburban semis. The point to be made is that description is subjective. It is, to a degree, built on the sensitivities of the writer and it must be remembered that the agents' task is to sell.

Those who sell anything – beef cubes, motor cars or washing machines – are restricted by statute on what they can claim for their products. Nevertheless, salesmen of every kind suffer from an illness which might be called congenital hyperbole. Residential estate agents are no exception; in recent years, their commercial colleagues have put a new meaning on the word 'prestigious'. At one time, prestigious meant showy in a rather false kind of way. Nowadays, it means – or agents think it means – something pretty damned fine which will bloat the tenant's ego, if not his profits, to an extravagant pitch. Trade descriptions are controlled. Misrepresentation is a crime. But, if an estate agent's personal taste persuades him that a house is beautiful, is he wrong to describe it in that way – knowing that somebody, somewhere, whose tastes are quite different, will regard it as absolutely ghastly?

It is the task of the estate agent to make the best of that bad job we were talking about. Only the late lamented Roy Brooks got away with down-to-earth honesty in his advertising. During the period from 1950 to 1971, the Roy Brooks advertisements became compulsory reading in the property columns of *The Sunday Times* and *Observer*. They contained a soft mix of what his successors describe as candour and humour and his style proved an immensely successful formula for the selling of houses. When describing a house overlooking a golf course, Roy Brooks included the phrase: 'Prospect of elderly gentlemen looking for their balls in the rough'. Here are some examples of Roy Brooks' style:

ONE OF THE FILTHIEST HOUSES I'VE SEEN FOR A LONG TIME. A crumbling corner PERIOD RES. There are many things that can be said about FASHIONABLE PIMLICO: Dingy, for instance. 9 rms (some quite fine altho' they've kept coal in a bedrm & the Drawing rm chimney piece is sprawled across the flr.) Built in an age of elegance, contemporary I should think, with Emperor LOUIS PHILIPPE, to restore it is about the only challenge left to a rich young couple today. ONLY £8,450. Lse 80 yrs. G.R. ONLY £70.

WANTED: Someone with taste, means and a stomach strong enough to buy this erstwhile house of ill-repute in Pimlico. It is untouched by the 20th Century as far as convenience for even the basic human decencies is concerned. Although it reeks of damp or worse, the plaster is coming off the walls and daylight peeps through a hole in the roof, it is still habitable judging by the bed of rags, fag ends and empty bottles in one corner. Plenty of scope for the socially aspiring to express their decorative taste and get their abode in 'The Glossy' and nothing to stop them putting Westminster on their notepaper. 10 rather unpleasant rooms with slimy back yard. £4,650 Freehold. Tarted up, these houses make £15,000.

WILL ANYONE TAKE PITY ON A NASTY OLD HOUSE adj. REGENT'S PK. TER. On still nights the friendly howl of Hyaena floats over the Mappin terraces & one can, maybe, imagine oneself far away from our acquisitive society. 9 rms., 2 bathrms., kit. All in pretty foul order. Will only sell for single occupancy to gentle-people. G.R. £70. Lse. abt. 75 yrs. £7,250 (I expect we'll see it resold, done up, in a year or so for abt. £14,000).

Roy Brooks became, apart from everything else, a television personality and, as his fame grew, he took to addressing his readers – and, my goodness, they were legion – on matters of moment. He expressed views about Vietnam which most of us felt but hadn't the nerve to say publicly and he was complaining about apartheid long before complaint about it became really fashionable. For example, this appeared as a 'property wanted' ad:

LADY B WRITES: *'I want future home: somewhere like Norfolk, spacious, rambling, dilapidated – needing care (derelict if 2 rooms habitable) . . . ready to take in young nieces and nephews from Africa when the upheaval is sparked off.'* Unexpected disasters are bad enough, but avoidable ones even worse. Effective, full-blooded sanctions that are carried out against Rhodesia/S.Africa, whatever the cost, are cheaper than the loss of a single life of either colour – but I'm no expert – just prefer people alive rather than dead – politically free rather than imprisoned. I suggest you all send ten bob, one year's sub to ANTI-APARTHEID NEWS, 89 Charlotte St. W1.

He only occasionally mentioned room sizes by expressing precise dimensions, but his words were enough: 'small third bedroom for child or dwarf lodger'. He often put greater emphasis on the people who owned houses than on the houses themselves:

> **FASHIONABLE CHELSEA.** Fine 8 rm. house. 2 bathrooms. Consent to let rms. (Estimated income £1,500 p.a. plus owner's suite; 3 gd. rms.) £3,000 spent bringing up to her own high standards by friend of Royalty. (Trekked 800 miles on horseback with 100 bearers & baby brother in meat safe to make African camp for Edward, Prince of Wales, & took *'elevenses'* – stewed duck served in chamberpot, with Great Queen Magui, aged 102, 13 husbands – 2 thrown by herself to the crocodiles, & who had tin of sardines & Golden Syrup on the table to show how English she was . .) Lse. 10 yrs. Thought renewable. G.R. only £20 p.a. £7,995, try ANY offer.

It was all great knockabout stuff. I suspect that Roy Brooks would have had a bad time with the Property Misdescriptions Act. Many have tried – unsuccessfully – to follow his style but, in truth, most estate agents show little imagination in their description of houses for sale and one wonders what the politicians are really on about.

In fact, agents have a schizophrenic attitude to description. On the one hand, their advertising – which is mightily expensive – has to produce the maximum return. So they economise by contracting description to an often incomprehensible level: 'S-D HSE, 2.5 BEDS, 2 R, K & B, INT. GGE, LGE GDN, FT TS, CLO S & B, £42,500, MGE AVLE, STS.'

This means, of course, that what we have here is a semi-detached house which contains two rooms into which you might conceivably get a bed and one which would be better used as a broom cupboard or paint store. There are two reception rooms, a kitchen and a bathroom. There is an integral garage (which means it is keeping the rest of the house up and, if the car bursts into flames, the chances of saving even the cat are remote). There is a large garden (and large might mean different things to different people) which contains fruit trees, perhaps an ancient Bramley which bears diseased apples intermittently. It is close to a station and buses, or shops and buses, or schools and buses, according to what was in the compiler's mind when he wrote it. The price is clear, but will have gone up before the advertisement appears, and the rest means that a mortgage is available subject to status.

The printers of newspapers – the chaps who actually set all this stuff in type before the presses roll – are often quite good at correcting the spelling mistakes of copywriters. But only as long as they understand the language. Faced with

contracted descriptions which are variable depending on their source, they can often make mistakes which, on the face of it, are just as intelligible as the original. The most famous is 'COTTAGE, BAT, SN LGE AT REAR', which was meant to convey that the cottage was built of brick and tile with a sun lounge at the rear. It was printed as

'COTTAGE, BATS IN LGE', which is hardly a selling point.

Contracted expression of this kind would scarcely have appealed to Sir Arthur Quiller-Couch, but economy in advertising demands the practice. The problem is that no one seems to have written a contracted vocabulary for house agents so that all can convey the same meaning to an already baffled public. The even fairly obvious contractions like 'DBLE B/RMS' could mean double bathrooms, as opposed to bedrooms, to those who have wide experience. There is a house in Knightsbridge with his and hers facing WCs – which brings a new dimension to togetherness.

One of residential agency's really upmarket firms developed a system of pictorial representation of what houses contained, rather like the motorway signs which tell you that you have to drive another 57 miles if you actually want steak and chips because the sign is devoid of a knife and fork: it has only a cup and petrol pump, and there is nothing more depressing when it's raining and you're hungry than that missing knife and fork. Anyway, this upmarket firm dreamed up these little drawings, presumably because they realised that their upper crust clients sometimes have difficulty reading long words like 'bedroom' and 'reception'. The agents don't seem to do it so much these days which is surprising, bearing in mind the government's concern about the decline in reading standards.

So let us, for the sake of the sanity of future generations, establish standard contractions:

H	house
B	bungalow
F	flat
Rec.	reception room
Bd	bedroom

Bt	bathroom (Bt (Bd) might stand for a bidet in the bathroom but that's probably carrying sophistication too far)
K	kitchen
G	garage
G × 2	double garage
CP	car port
GCH	gas fired central heating
OCH	oil fired central heating

– and now you make up the rest. Somebody should issue an edict – perhaps the Office of Fair Trading – requiring estate agents to follow the standard list. Advertisements which said: 'B, 2 rec, 3 bd, bt, k, g, GCH – £45,000,' would mean something to all of us.

As opposed to the economy practised in advertising, the art of description comes into its own in house agents' detailed particulars of sale. These are the particulars sent to anxious buyers in response to their requests for details of properties of a particular kind at a particular price. The fact that the detailed particulars never quite correspond with the anxious buyers' briefs is dealt with elsewhere. What they get is description which, on the face of it, has to be treated with deep suspicion. The agent is, after all, trying his best to sell something. His description is therefore probably rich in adjectives, generous in its interpretation of dimensions and glowing in its appreciation of individual features which normally have the appeal of an over-occupied pigsty.

Description – which has caused so much anger and complaint – will re-appear as we run through the process of house transfer.

4 THE PROCESS

As has been said, people don't buy and sell their houses, bungalows and flats all that frequently. They are, therefore, inexpert and inexperienced in the procedures of sale or purchase. Inexperience brings doubt, uncertainty and anxiety and, when the going gets as rough as the going can get, these emotions tip over the edge into deep neurosis. People – normal, healthy people with dogs and loveable little ways – tend to suffer serious character change in the process of house transfer whether buying or selling. Happily but newly married couples embarking on a first-time purchase of what they hope will be a blissful love nest all too frequently end up in the divorce courts. Sellers, through the frustrations of delay, misunderstanding and occasional professional incompetence, have been known to throw boots and valuable vases through their own windows.

In the middle of all this mayhem is the estate agent. Beside or behind him – and, sometimes, under his feet or riding on his back – are others such as the building society manager, endowment insurance salesman, structural surveyor and lawyers for both sides of the transaction. In order to encounter all of these strange and occasionally bewildering characters, let us run through a typical house transfer. It would be wrong to suggest all sales and purchases are like this: as an example, it is extreme because everything – well, almost everything – that might go wrong has been included. It is also unlikely that buyers and sellers will come across anyone quite like the estate agents, lawyers or any of the others in this tale of woe.

(Indeed, it is unlikely that estate agents and lawyers will come across buyers and sellers who in any way resemble those I have described – not often, anyway.) As they say in the preface to those searing novels of human lust and passion, the characters are products of the author's imagination and any resemblance to absolutely anyone, either living or dead, is purely coincidental. And we all know the truth of that!

For the sake of good order and proper progression, we will assume that the story starts with the instruction from a seller. The expert will know that this is slightly false, because the estate agent will already have been busying himself with his list of applicants, other properties for sale and those properties on which a sale has already been agreed. All of this would be quite enough for any normal person, but agents love new instructions. They are his life-blood. Without instructions, his shelves are barren and his phone almost silent.

The seller will be selling for any one of a dozen reasons. His home may no longer be large enough for either his growing family or, perhaps, his ego; he may have been transferred to Wick or Devizes by his employer; his wife may have left him and expressed a burning desire, with some judicial support, for half the proceeds of sale; he may have decided to go and live in one of those retirement complexes – or even the Costa del this or that. The sale may be a forced one – a foreclosure by a building society, a bank or an insurance company, either because repayments have slipped or because the owner's business has collapsed round his ears and his house has been used as collateral. The reason for sale will dictate the urgency and the level of neurosis enjoyed by the seller.

The first hint of an instruction will often be in the form of a telephone call, the *I've got this house to sell, haven't I? I've been trying to sell it myself, but it's getting a bit urgent now* kind of telephone call. Our friendly neighbourhood estate agent will pick up quite a lot of information from those first few words, even before he has seen the place he is supposed to sell. First of all, the seller is one of those clever boots who doesn't much like estate agents and does everything, but everything, himself. The chances are, therefore, that the house will be full of off-level shelves, unsafe wiring and plumbing and central heating systems that groan sadly to themselves in the night, waking children and dogs and terrifying the cat. He knows the type well. But, so avid is he for instructions, he will take all that in his stride. Secondly, he will note with a deep sigh that, however inexpertly it may have been handled, the house has been on the market for some time. In normal economic conditions, a house that has been on the market for some time will have developed a reputation as a no-go area – a kind of semi-detached leprosy. Our friendly neighbourhood estate agent will know that he will have to work twice as hard to persuade buyers to view it.

He will, nevertheless, fix an appointment to call on the vendor. His purpose will be to count the number of rooms, measure their sizes, keep a wary eye open for the more apparent defects, suffer deep shock at the appearance of the front garden and the general decorative condition and make notes which will help him to draft his detailed particulars of sale. Before his appointment with the vendor, he will have grabbed the office camera (which never seems to have a film in it when he needs to use it) to take a photograph or two of this disastrous pile from the best vantage point. He will also discuss price with the seller and explain in words of one syllable what his terms are, leaving a written explanation of those terms, amended or otherwise, so that the owner can spend the next few days grumbling about them.

Most estate agents will take a tape measure or rule to measure the room sizes. Unless he also takes a reliable assistant, there is risk of error. If he asks the anxious vendor to hold the other end of the tape, the risk of error becomes dangerously high – after all, and you will remember this from an earlier chapter, the vendor is anxious to sell. If the impression is given that the rooms are just a bit bigger than 10 feet × 10 feet, so much the better. Some estate agents rely on the length of their shoes and do a kind of balancing act along each wall. This method is not entirely satisfactory, because most houses for sale are still furnished at the time the instructions are given. Dodging the commode or the mass of occasional tables can add or subtract inches and, sometimes, even feet to or from room dimensions. It is also irritating to the estate agent to realise that he is wearing a new pair of heavy brogues for the first time and that he hasn't the slightest idea of their exact length.

Attendance at premises for the purposes of taking instructions, measurements and description seems a fairly straightforward activity; in fact, it is fraught with difficulty. The estate agent has to do his job but, at the same time, develop friendly relations with the vendor, create mutual confidence and, generally, give the impression that he knows what he is doing. And by the way, although estate agents are usually referred to as 'he' throughout this book, remember that there are just as many 'shes' in the business – and most of them make better estate agents than their menfolk. So the estate agent has to be charming and reassuring. He has to appear confident that he can sell the place and hint at the dozens, even hundreds, of applicants on his list who will beat a path to the door of this desirable residence. At the same time, he has to be realistic and somehow, without mortifying the vendor, point out ways in which the proud owner might increase the speed and value of the sale.

Some estate agents who well understand the sensitivities of this stage of the proceedings have produced little leaflets which offer advice to budding vendors. Take, for example, the matter of odour. Houses which have been lived in for a decade or two develop their own smells which reflect the lifestyle of the owners, their families and their pets. Some houses take your breath away in more ways than one. The heavy mixture of boiled cabbage, wet washing hanging from the airer in the kitchen and old Fido on his rug in the corner can unquestionably put vendors off. The estate agent has to point these things out to the proud owner in such a way that he or she won't be so offended that the agent is sent off with a flea in his ear and, in some cases, other parts of his person.

Small defects should be remedied: the window in the downstairs loo which has been cracked for fourteen years really ought to be repaired; the damp patch on the ceiling which resulted from an unfortunate accident with little Willie's potty might respond happily to a coat of emulsion; and that wall cupboard in the kitchen which comes forward at an angle if you put into it more than two tins of Spam really

should be braced. Some people live in an extraordinary muddle which, to them, is home. Muddle might be endearing to some who regard it merely as homeliness, but the muddle or mess is certainly not endearing to every potential buyer. Children's toys, as we all know, spread all over every house. A much-loved, one-eared teddy bear has an obvious appeal lying on a pretty counterpane in the nursery, but one roller skate abandoned on the stairs can bring both disaster and a third party claim.

Pets have an instinct about potential buyers. They seem to realise that the serenity of their lives is about to be disturbed by Mr and Mrs Portly and their unruly offspring on whom their owners are lavishing more attention than seems necessary or natural. Little Willie, whose potty caused that damp patch on the ceiling, has to be persuaded not to show off his pet tarantula or invite Mrs Portly to stroke Riggles, the homely rock python. Old Fido, who looks and smells like an unkempt rug, must be relegated to the garden shed because he is likely to become emotional. He will either bite someone or insist on making passionate love to Mrs Portly's left leg, the one with the varicose veins. At best, he will ladder her elastic stocking and the worst doesn't bear thinking about.

The garden gives a first and lasting impression. A suggestion that the proud owner might actually cut the grass, hoe what might laughingly be called the borders and remove the rusting car parts, old bedsteads and other domestic detritus will not be warmly received. The estate agent may have to explain with forelock-touching humility that a payment of £20 or so to some horny-handed son of the soil to make the garden look reasonably trim could easily add £200 or more to the sale price.

So long as she gets on reasonably well with Fido, and there can be no certainty about that, mother-in-law should also be relegated to the garden shed when potential buyers call to view. Mothers-in-law tend to over-sell, given half a chance. Our Jimmy, she will say, has put a lot of work into the place, she can't think why he's moving and she hopes whoever buys it deserves such an absolute palace. This kind of thing makes everyone uncomfortable – including the estate agent who, you will remember, is still deeply concerned about the do-it-yourself electric wiring and the central heating that groans in the night.

All of this and more will be exercising the estate agent's mind when he is taking instructions. He will be making copious notes to help him to compile his detailed particulars of sale – where the power points are, for example – wondering at the same time if it is actually possible to fit a plug to the one that is now behind the radiator fixed as an afterthought by the same do-it-yourself vendor. The location of fitted cupboards, wardrobes; whether there is an immersion heater and does it work; and is the loft accessible to people other than highly-trained members of the SAS – all of these things have to be noted.

And then we come to the task of pricing. The estate agent will be aware of the prices at which other similar houses have changed hands in the area. He will know if the market is rising, falling or sitting uneasily on a plateau. He will know what the demand is like; and the wise and efficient agent will know enough about the local economy to judge if there are about to be massive redundancies in the local staple industry or whether new industry is about to surge into the town and mop up the unemployed. He will know, too, about planning and development proposals and roughly when the threatened by-pass will be constructed within ten feet of the front door.

The estate agent faces something of a dilemma when he is pricing a house. Obviously, he wants to sell it, because until he does, he receives no fee. Although the fee is related to the sale price he achieves, he would rather sell at a realistic price than hold out for a higher figure which might never be offered. He also has to take into account what the owner wants. In boom times, owners believe what they read in the papers and add noughts on to their prices accordingly. In bad times, the owner may be caught in a price trap because he may have paid through the nose for the house in the first place and have a mortgage higher than the current sale value. Our friendly neighbourhood estate agent, full of wisdom and nodding sagely, will try to guide the anxious owner from pious hope to pragmatic realism.

And don't forget that the estate agent has to spell out his terms. This is a legal requirement, and the vendor has to be absolutely clear about the instructions he gives and the appointment he makes to achieve a sale. Practice varies in different parts of the country and it is worth running through the range of possibilities. A later chapter will deal in depth with the letter of the law and some of the practices which have developed where agency, financing and legal functions are provided under one roof. But, for the time being, we will stick with the anxious vendor who desperately wants to sell.

You will remember that, in our example, the vendor had already tried, and had so far failed, to sell his property himself. Do-it-yourself estate agency can be successful and it would be wrong to dismiss it. A survey some time ago showed that 12 per cent of house sales were achieved through friends, relatives, an advertisement in the local paper or a hand-painted 'For Sale' board just inside the front gate. The cost was nil except in the case of the advertisement, which might cost £30 or £40, and the hand-painted 'For Sale' board, the cost of which depends on what you have available in the garden shed. The problem about doing it yourself is that you have a much narrower potential client base and, if percentage rules are applied, the chances of sale are greatly reduced. Nevertheless, for a cost of, say, £40 or less, it is worth a try – but don't forget our friendly agent's reaction when his vendor told him that he had been trying to sell: the house had been available for some time and might have developed that semi-detached leprosy. Much will depend on the vendor's time scale. If a speedy sale is vital, an agent should be quicker. Although there are no fixed fee scales – which would be contrary to the principles of our competitive society – there is a sameness about fees. It should, nevertheless, always be possible to haggle a bit and much will depend on the market in a particular area, the competition and whether there is a strong demand for your kind of property. The power to haggle is strongest if you, as a vendor, follow the path of sole agency.

Sole agency in the south of England will cost between one and two per cent of the selling price. If you are the proud owner of a house worth, say, £100,000, two per cent will cost you £2,000 plus VAT and one per cent a mere £1,000 plus VAT. Sole agency means that you apppoint one agent only and in many parts of the country, particularly the north of England, agents will only accept instructions as sole agents. You can put a time limit on a sole agency appointment; this is often a satisfactory means of ensuring that the agent takes you and your sale seriously.

Joint sole agency – the appointment of two agents and no more – slightly weakens your haggling power but extends your potential buyer catchment. Agents might ask for another half per cent for a joint sole agency appointment. The agents will settle their own fee arrangements between themselves. So far as you are concerned, it is no sale – no fee and you will pay your fee to whichever agent produces the buyer. A joint sole agency costs the same as if you gave multiple instructions on a no sale – no fee basis and multiple instructions increase your potential buyer catchment as widely as it can be flung. The sensible choice is therefore between sole agency, if you feel parsimonious about fees, and multiple agency, if you want to get the thing moving. In certain markets, sole agency can get things moving rather quicker anyway.

One or two words of warning should be heeded. Most agents will ask the vendor to sign a form of instruction primarily to confirm that he understands the terms of business. Make sure, if you are a vendor, that you know what you will get for your money. The agent should produce, within the fee which has been agreed, the detailed particulars of sale, the card with photographs for his shop window, reference to your property in one or more block advertisements in appropriate newspapers and, of course, the sale board. These are standard services in the south of England. Elsewhere, there might be an extra charge and, certainly, advertising is almost always charged as an extra. You might also be charged for accompanied viewings. The point of saying all this is that you, if you are a vendor, should find out precisely the service to be provided.

Before the vendor signs the instructions chit, he should read it. Beware of the phrase 'sole selling rights', which is quite different from sole agency. It means that, even if you sold eventually to your rich uncle from Canberra who had never heard of the agent, you might still have to pay a fee. Also be wary of the phrase: 'in the event of our introducing a buyer who is able and willing to complete the transaction'. This is a particularly dangerous provision in the case of multiple agency or if you change your mind and decide to stay put after all, circumstances which are not uncommon.

So the agent jumps into his executive motor car or, these days, onto his bike, having measured everything, settled a price, made notes for his sale particulars, informed the vendor of his rights and taken a photograph or two. He returns to his office in a creative frenzy, licks his pencil, but doesn't necessarily begin immediately to compose the pearls of prose which will describe the house he has just left. If he is an astute estate agent, he will, in the case of multiple instructions, immediately telephone two or three applicants on his list whom the property might suit. His voice will take on a confidential almost conspiratorial air, you know the kind of thing:

'I've just been instructed on a house which matches your needs precisely – no, there aren't even particulars of sale yet but, if you ring the owner, he'll show you round straight away – and watch out for the dog'. In boom times, this is common practice and often results in a sale without even the trouble of preparing detailed particulars or having the films developed. Even in bad times, it is worth a try. Apart from anything else, it impresses the vendor.

5 THE PROCESS CONTINUES

So we have signed an instruction and our friendly estate agent has already urged one or two special applicants to inspect the property. He will have no great optimism about the results. He has to prepare his particulars of sale which he will circulate to the other applicants on his list and illustrate with the least disastrous photograph of those he has taken. He will have a larger print developed to enhance the cogent little message on the card, which he will place in his shop window. He will arrange for the erection of a 'For Sale' board of the right legal dimensions. Depending on the value of the house, he will decide whether to have mini-prints supplied from his negative or whether merely to photocopy the print he already has, after sticking it on his particulars.

These are big decisions: it will cost much more in both time and real money to stick mini-prints on to printed particulars. In a sizeable estate agency office, there might be as many as 200 applicants which the property might suit – and young Myrtle never sticks the photographs on straight the first time anyway. She ends up in tears and the morale of the office is destroyed for a week. The window card is an entirely different matter. Although the world and his wife will never admit it, they are chronically myopic, so the description on the window card must be terse and writ large but, at the same time, indicate size, price, neighbourhood and general composition. The photograph must be as large as the card and the window will allow. And then he has to compose the advertisement for the press. It's all go, as they say.

Our estate agent sucks his pencil and begins the wearisome task of composing those pearls of prose which will send dozens of anxious buyers to view this desirable residence. We have already put the blame for estate agents' prose on George Robins, and we have hinted at the state of the law which inhibits the wilder excesses of description. Our estate agent is not a Roy Brooks with a non-buying readership as large as Wilbur Smith's. Neither is he a George Bernard Shaw, but he does have the Office of Fair Trading peeking over his shoulder like an angry schoolmaster holding a large and heavy ruler with which to rap knuckles at the hint of an excessive adjective. Worse, he has done it all before and there is a limit to his ingenuity, particularly if vivid writing is forbidden. After all, it is his commissioned task to sell the place. Quite apart from that, if his description of the house has the sales appeal of pork pies well past their sell-by dates, he won't even get the approval of the vendor to what he has written. The vendor will want the script worked up into a Cecil B de Mille production. You will understand our estate agent's problems: the end result pleases nobody and the recipients of this turgid, uninspiring description lurch into even deeper lethargy, probably giving up altogether the idea of moving.

Description is never easy. It is said that the British communicate mostly in slang and clichés and some estate agents have

taken certain words as their own, no matter what they mean. Take the word 'bijou', for example: as a noun, it means a trinket, a jewel or a little box; as an adjective, it means small and elegant. If the agent, who invariably uses the word as an adjective, meant that his bijou residence was a little box, it would never offend the Office of Fair Trading. To describe a two up, one down, with no bathroom or kitchen as bijou is getting very close to a reprimand. The word 'immaculate' is irresistible to some estate agents; it means spotless, unstained, pure. How many second-hand homes are spotless, unstained, pure? Even immediately after decoration, it is as likely as not that you scrape the wall as you are putting the ladder away –

and then there are the depredations perpetrated by little Willie and his potty, Fido the dog and even a bored goldfish who can, with a flick of his tail, splash unchanged water over the wallpaper. The local amenities such as schools, shops and buses must also be described. If the shops are labelled as ten minutes away, one has to ask by whose standards – Granny or Nigel Mansell on a good day? And those schools which are so conveniently placed, are they akin to St Trinian's? Has one been called the Nelson Mandela Comprehensive by some recalcitrant local authority which only employs left-wing militants as teachers?

All of this is very taxing stuff, but there is worse to come. To whom does our estate agent send the completed particulars? Most estate agents' offices are now computerised. There is a wide range of systems on the market and, although it may not be apparent, sophistication has crept into agency service. Nevertheless, the systems don't make judgements beyond their own powers of logic and we have already indicated that logic is not much in evidence among the house selling and house buying public. No system has been devised which can take proper account of human whim, so our estate agent has to use his own fertile imagination to decide distribution.

It is, of course, pertinent to ask how these lists of houses for sale and anxious applicants are created in the first place. We have already seen how one instruction has come to the agent, but one instruction is not going to send the agent to the Bahamas for his holidays, even if he sells the house before one of his competitors. There are all kinds of tricks to build up a portfolio of homes for sale. Unless he is one of the national 'country houses, castles and landed estates' agents, the estate agent serves a single town or patch of a conurbation. He knows his patch well; he knows every street, close and alley and, because he is street-wise and active in the market-place, he knows about pricing. He also knows his competitors. To keep his knowledge up-to-date, he will spend some time every week patrolling his patch in what might have been the firm's car before the Chancellor of the Exchequer imposed his swingeing 'car benefit' provisions; now, it could be a bicycle or even his feet. He will make careful notes about competitors' boards outside houses and home-made boards erected by those optimists who think they can do it themselves.

And what does he do with this information? Well, it has to be said that some estate agents are pretty sneaky. Most of them buy every year a copy of the Register of Electors – a tiny investment for a document of immense value. The Register lists everybody (unless the Electoral Registration Officer was inept, which sometimes happens) and it is a handy reference when an estate agent wants to write a personal note to a seller who has instructed somebody else. 'Dear Mr and Mrs Smith', writes our agent, who is wise enough to know that, if you want to get anywhere at all in the house-selling business, Mrs Smith has to be brought into the act as quickly as possible, 'we have several keen applicants who have been disappointed recently because the (house/bungalow/flat) in your (street/avenue/crescent/close) was bought by another buyer. I notice that your house (bungalow/flat) is on the market. It would give me the greatest pleasure to receive your instructions so that I can pass the details to the many people on our list who would be very interested. Our terms of business are . . .'. Mr and Mrs Smith, if the agent is lucky, may already be beyond the neurosis level and the offer of a string of disappointed potential buyers to be directed towards them might be almost irresistible.

There is nothing sneaky about this if it happens to be true; but it rarely is. To the agent, this is merely an act of faith on two counts. First, somewhere among his list of applicants, there might conceivably be someone whom this house (bungalow/flat) might suit, but he is unlikely to check before he sends out the letter. Secondly, in the course of the next few days, a previously unheard of applicant will appear in his office whose requirements match the house (bungalow/flat) precisely.

There are other tricks used by agents to gain instructions, such as the 'board' game. There is now statutory control over agents' boards, which we will come to later. But at one time, houses for sale could be hidden by the cluster of 'For Sale' boards outside them for months as a result of multiple agency instructions. Some unscrupulous agents would simply slip their board into the cluster even if they had not been instructed and rely on standard odds that they would be the agent to be telephoned by a hopeful buyer. Large blocks of flats are particularly liable to this treatment. No individual owner knew to which flat a board referred; nor did any potential buyer. Buyers were therefore bound to telephone all the agents. If a call came to the agent who had slipped his board into the cluster when no one was looking and didn't have any instructions anyway, he was full of apologies. The flat had just that morning been sold – but how lucky the caller was. He had just been instructed to sell a similar flat in an equally prestigious (that word again) block just 200 yards away. Or why not a house with a garden where the kids can play and Fido can bury his bones?

No, well, leave it to me, I will try to find you a flat in that particular block which you like so much.

How does he do that? How does he know which flat is available in a block of sixty? Well, it is not difficult to slip a few fictional names and addresses into competitors' systems so that all their detailed particulars of sale land in a neat pile on our sneaky agent's desk. So common did this practice become that some agents stopped disclosing addresses on their details in order that other agents could not call on the owner directly. But, as we now know, our particular agent knows all about his patch; as likely as not, he will be able to identify the house from a photograph no matter how blurred it might be.

Psychology comes into the dirty tricks department. Imagine, if you will, a road of, say, a hundred houses, all much the same except where a rugged individualist has added an ornate canopy over the front door or, indeed, a complete porch or where a member of an ethnic minority has painted all the walls bright orange. It happens: our friendly estate agent notices a few 'For Sale' boards appearing in the road – not his, but those of a competitor or, worse, several competitors. When neighbours indicate that they are about to move house, particularly for reasons of self-aggrandisement, Mrs House-owner becomes peevish and restless. She begins to put pressure on Mr House-owner, who has probably become peevish and restless himself for exactly the same reasons. If they then receive a letter of this *'Oh dear, we have this disappointed applicant'* kind, they are pushed gently towards a move. If the letter goes on to say that, on the agent's lists, there is a wide selection of houses at bargain prices with full mortgage facilities available, they are on the phone in a trice. In that case, the agent picks up both a vendor and a potential buyer, and he probably hasn't even bothered to check his computer listing at all. He just relies on the basic human need to keep up with the Joneses wherever they might be going.

There are also tricks to attract applicants. Although instructions to sell are vital to the success of an estate agency business, it is also necessary to have applicants who seriously want to buy. The agent can, of course, advertise – and nearly all of them do. Whole pages of property advertisements appear in the local, regional and national press and in the glossy magazines. These can cost hundreds, sometimes thousands, of pounds every week, but they attract applicants who will, as we know, probably buy something completely different from the house which was advertised and attracted their interest in the first place. However, there are other ways to pick up applicants.

Some agents have gone so far as to subscribe for an additional unlisted telephone line to their office. The line is never used for outgoing calls except in dire emergency. It is there to receive calls in response to advertisements placed by the agent which read 'Pleasant three-bed house in Pinner (or wherever), large garden, good dec. order. Owner must sell – so low price. £85,000. No agents. Ring XXX YYYY'. Whoever answers the phone when it rings only gives the number;

one agent actually had typed instructions above the telephone so that there would not be a slip. 'Oh, we have just had an offer which I must discuss with my husband/wife but give me your name, address, and telephone number and I will get back to you'. Bingo! Another applicant, keen enough to be scrutinising the papers and keen enough to ring; and that applicant will go into the system and, to his or her surprise perhaps, begin to receive wads of detailed particulars of sale. And, being human, they will read them – and might just be persuaded.

One firm of estate agents negotiated with at least twenty suppliers of household hardware and domestic services in the locality to give substantial, but widely variable, discounts to applicants completing a purchase through that firm. The vouchers were printed off in handy little booklets and, guess what, a modest discount was offered on the agent's fees when the buyer wanted to sell his property at some time in the future. The poor buyer was still arguing with his wife about the choice of wallpaper for that house, without worrying about the next one. But that particular device was attractive to applicants and resulted in rather more applicants on the agent's list at a time when applicants were important and hard to come by. It was not surprising: all the discounts, valued at something over £500 if all the vouchers were used, related to the kind of purchases people make when they first move into a house.

It would be wrong to suggest that all agents get up to tricks of this kind. Many rely on strong corporate identities, reputation, sponsorship of football teams and, of course, gimmicks. In the last category, one agent, a hot air balloon fanatic, had his firm's name all over his toy as he drifted across his operational territory. Estate agents also have themselves listed in Yellow Pages, directories, official town guides and on posters at bus stops and railway stations. Good estate agents are also, in many towns, pillars of the establishment and speak at meetings of the Rotary Club and Round Table. In fact, so respectable are so many of the breed that it is difficult to imagine how the rotten image has arisen.

While we are on the subject of utter respectability, it is probably worth diverting our attention for a moment to those agents who act for the blue-blooded fraternity, or those who are just plain rich. The big house market out in the country – the country estates, the Elizabethan manors, the occasional castle – is served by a relatively small number of national agents. Some of them have local branches, but most of them have offices in Mayfair and are staffed by young gentlemen called Nigel, Adrian and Rupert and young ladies called Fiona and Felicity. As firms, they can be seen at the Game Fair and they sponsor horse races, appear at point-to-points and attend and even participate in three-day events at the right places. When the aristocracy want to sell a house, they think instinctively of one or other of the big agency names.

If, as a potential vendor, you happen to be in this category, you will find that a different system applies. Splendid houses, often steeped in real or imagined history, demand special treatment. You don't sell Woburn Abbey from a two-paged detailed particulars of sale and badly developed photographs taken on a stormy day. (No, so far as I know, Woburn Abbey is not for sale; it's only an example.) Stately homes of this kind justify a brochure which contains not one, but several, exterior and interior photographs, preferably taken by Lord Lichfield or Lord Snowdon, and layout plans of the house, the gardens and whatever else the estate consists of. They also justify colour advertising in the best newspapers and at least a page or two in *Country Life*. Because the agents hob-nob with the gentry most of the time, they are party to all the tittle-tattle about forthcoming marriages, pending divorces, unofficial engagements which are likely to last, deaths, of course, and the occasional affair which could lead to trouble. This is intelligence of extraordinary value to the agent. He is also aware that the aristocracy is not as rich as it was, so he has to keep his finger on the needs of Middle Eastern potentates and all those Patels who will become multi-millionaires in the next few months.

A percentage fee of one or two per cent on a £2 million house and estate works out at between £20,000 and £40,000. A fee of that size, even at the top end, has no real relevance to a vendor bent on selling at £2 million. It probably has even less relevance to the buyer who might just as well have paid £2,100,000 for his status symbol. The fees charged for sales of this kind are therefore likely to be three per cent. In addition, the vendor will be expected to pay in advance for the agent's expenditure on that thrilling brochure with all those expensive photographs, the extensive and expensive advertising and a new pair of green wellies for Fiona to wear at the next point-to-point.

Fees and costs of this kind would send our friendly local estate agent into paroxysms of delight. However, selling country estates is not easy, nor is it quick. The best of the agents working at this level will take time on negotiation to ensure that their clients obtain the best possible price, enough to justify their fees and those incidental expenses. Unlike our local agents, they are not in the numbers game, seeking their profits from high turnover on suburban semis and ready to recommend a startling price reduction to secure a sale. There are, as you might expect, fewer complaints about agents' incompetence at this level of the market, although they still arise.

It is, nevertheless, true that the marketing of country estates brings its problems. The composition of selling copy demands careful research. There is every chance that Queen Elizabeth did actually sleep there; battles may have been waged in the meadow by the river; and you can make what you will of that brown stain in the priest's hole behind the fireplace in the fourth drawing room. The measurement of a house with 120 rooms takes a bit of time and, as in most old houses, there is risk of disaster. Feet, legs and whole torsos can go through rotten floor boards in the closed east wing. One well-known top people's agent, inspecting an empty ancient pile, inadvertently locked himself in a distant lavatory and it took four hours of patient work with a nail file before he regained his freedom. It is not recorded whether or not he was on an hourly rate and charged the vendor for the mishap.

There is one thing above all which sets ancestral homes apart from the run-of-the-mill semi and that is ghosts. Run-of-the-mill semis can, occasionally, sport a poltergeist or two and some even have an atmosphere which emanates from something other than boiled cabbage or old Fido. But if it is the ghost of some long dead ancestor you are after, you generally have to go to an ancestral home for it. Some ancestral homes are chock full of ghosts and, moreover, the vendor of the ancient pile which the agent is expected to sell seems to be on speaking terms with all of them. 'I can't think' remarks Lady So-and-So, in that off-hand manner people normally reserve for the weather, 'what Sir Horace will say when he finds we've moved to Bermuda'. After searching enquiry, the agent discovers that Sir Horace passed away in 1642 and has been around ever since. He hadn't been allowed into wherever he was supposed to have gone because of some sordid affair with a parlourmaid, whom he was comforting at the time of his fatal seizure. The parlourmaid is still around, too, but she doesn't talk to anybody because she knows her place and hurriedly disappears through walls in her nightie to get to it.

This kind of thing is yet another dilemma for the selling agent. Most of us, I suspect, would rather not have a ghost in the house. Goodness knows, there is enough to worry about with the central heating bills, the Council Tax and whether the cesspool is going to overflow again when we have our next week-end house party. There are people, however, who think a ghost, tetchy though he may possibly be because of unfulfilled passion, is really rather a bonus. Does the agent mention Sir Horace and the maid, and any others who may be scurrying about the place, in the brochure and have the Office of Fair Trading down on him like a ton of bricks? No one in the Office of Fair Trading is allowed to believe in ghosts, particularly if they are written into brochures or detailed particulars of sale. So does our agent leave out any reference to them and raise the matter casually during the accompanied viewing? 'How are you with ghosts, Mr Patel (or Sheikh Abdul-el-Abba)? You see, Sir Horace is still about and it seems he won't, after all, want to go Bermuda without the parlourmaid. And she won't be able to go because Lady So-and-So is only taking a bungalow and already has a local staff'. Most agents in this upper-class category normally market top houses with ghosts to the Americans, who don't seem to mind them a bit. In fact, just the reverse, they love them. 'Gee Wilbur,' they say. 'You'll have to come over to Stratford to meet our genuine (pronounced 'genuyne') ghost, Sir Horace'.

It is, therefore, just as tough at the top. While all this has been going on, our local estate agent has fed his data about the latest instruction into his computer. Size, location, price – all the details which, if he can remember to press all the right buttons, will produce a print-out of labels addressed to the applicants who have expressed a desire for this type of property. We have already learned that applicants, initially dogmatic about what they want, where they want it and how much it should cost, are fickle; knowing this, our agent presses a few more buttons and includes a few more applicants who, by now, have probably changed their minds anyway.

Nevertheless, some will wish to see the house. Our agent will not want his applicants making direct arrangements with the vendor unless he has sole agency. There is a risk that the vendor will sell through the competitor down the road, who has made it known that he will only charge three quarters of a per cent. Worse, the vendor might do a deal with the buyer whereby they both agree to be long lost cousins and bypass the luckless agent completely. After all, he has already done a lot of work. This kind of thing happens. Even disloyal staff have been known to take the particulars of an applicant and a house for sale, match the two together and take a half fee from the vendor who, because he has saved what could be as much as £1,000, is not going to rush off to the principal of the estate agency and complain.

In our example, however, everything is above board. The estate agent has made it clear, for the reasons given, that viewing should be strictly by appointment only, the arrangements to be made with his office. In the case of sole agency, the agent is sometimes less fussy and might allow visiting arrangements to be made directly with the vendor, so long as he believes that the vendor is disciplined enough to list all callers and do a thorough job of selling on his own. Listing callers is important because it is part of the agent's job to follow up, to chase and generally to make himself a thorough nuisance to the potential buyer.

Our agent is telephoned by his applicants who want to see the house. He will try to make the time to accompany the viewers, even in sole agency cases. There are several reasons for this, quite apart from the obvious one of keeping an eye on his commission. First, he will telephone the vendor to fix the time for the visit and to make sure the house is in a reasonable state for inspection, that the mother-in-law and Fido are in the potting shed and that the roller skates have been removed

from the stairs. Secondly, when potential buyers are looking over a property, it is best to keep Mr and Mrs Owner out of the way, if at all possible. Potential buyers are known to make remarks which could seriously affect the smooth running of a sale. Comments on the state of the garden start on arrival at the front gate, which the potential buyer notes is either already off its hinges or will be off by tomorrow. Faces will sag at the sight of the wallpaper in the hall that Mr and Mrs Owner

spent time and trouble choosing, because it reminded them of their honeymoon in Torremolinos. But we needn't go on, the point has been made. Buyers are not going to wax too enthusiastic anyway because, sooner or later, they are going to haggle about the price. But our agent will do his best to protect the owners from the worst of the comments; owners have been known to say that they wouldn't sell to that couple for a million, simply because the visitors didn't like the stair carpet.

Any estate agent will tell you that applicants are a strange lot. They have an absolute right to be strange. After all, they are receiving a service during which they might well be fawned over, driven about in motor cars to inspect other people's houses, given free cups of coffee and generally made a fuss of; and they are not asked to pay a penny for it. This extraordinary state of affairs comes about because the vendor foots the estate agent's bill. Yet a high proportion of complaints about the vendor of estate agents comes from applicants.

It is because the estate agent acts solely for the vendor that great misunderstanding can develop between him and his applicants. The agent will want to be sure that what he has before him is a genuine applicant and not a time-waster. Some people, bored to death with television, the kids or each other, have made a hobby out of looking at other people's houses. They have no intention of buying anything, but they tend to go for something a little up-market with a nice garden. If they make it past the gimlet eye of our astute estate agent, there is every chance that they will come away from the nice garden with a cutting or two which the bemused owner could not refuse for fear of losing a sale. Fortunately, these people are relatively rare.

People are funny like that. One large new estate of executive homes was advertised on the telly at prices well above what the average applicant could afford. The house builder who, clever Dick that he was, had decided he could handle his own marketing, was overwhelmed with crowds of people swarming over his show house, making grubby marks on the walls, dirtying and scuffing the carpets and pinching the plastic fruit as a souvenir. And not a single sale: the crowds had appeared 'because it was on the telly'. These, like those people who make a hobby out of gaping at others' houses, are time wasters and are disliked by estate agents just as much as agents are themselves disliked.

The estate agent will want to know the answers to several questions, which he will then enter on an applicant's card. Applicants have been known to rear up in the highest of dudgeons during this stage of the proceedings. Name, address and telephone number at home and at work are provided without a great deal of argument. Married? Children? Do you have a job? Oh, really! And how much do you earn a year? Wife working, is she? What does she get a week? Do you own the house you live in? You have a mortgage, I take it? How much outstanding? What society – and have they agreed to offer you a mortgage on a new place? To what limit? How do you propose to finance the difference? And what about HP debts?

Applicants have been known to ask, 'What's it got to do with you?' with all kinds of added expletives. In fact, it has quite a lot to do with the agent. If the housing market is buoyant, there could be a dozen people after the same house. Although the agent must pass on all the offers he receives to the vendor, his client, he is likely to be asked for his advice on the selection of the buyer. First-time buyers with no home to dispose of, good jobs with high disposable incomes, no children and no intention of having any for a few years and an offer from a building society because they have been saving with it for ages, are the most likely to be recommended. Without adequate information, the agent could be wasting his and his client's time. Applicants often arrive at an agent's office with no real idea of values, costs or monthly outgoings. Half are optimists and the other half are not. That other half are not exactly pessimists because pessimists don't usually bother to go to the estate agent's office anyway; but it is the optimists who usually know the least about their own capacity to meet the outgoings on a house they have set their hearts on.

Our friendly local estate-agent – and he does have to be friendly if he is to extract the information he needs – can, at this stage, act as counsellor to a hopeful buyer. He knows about value and, more importantly, he knows about outgoings. If he is to counsel well, he really does need the information he seeks. He will indicate the price level the applicant should aim for and therefore the size and location of the houses on the market at or about that price. Although he acts for the vendor, you just wouldn't believe it at this stage of the game. He gives the impression, at least, that he is looking only after the interests of the applicant. 'Have another cup of coffee while I am looking through my list of available property in your price range!'

Sometimes, an agent has to extract this information, to counsel and to provide details of houses for sale against the most difficult of circumstances. They are called children. Applicants who are doting parents and who have clearly practised a policy of free-expression bring their children into the agent's office, usually on a busy Saturday morning. After the first few moments of discreet enquiry and form filling, the children, bored and tetchy, climb down from their parents' laps. A local tornado would have less effect. It is even worse when doting parents have brought their dog, a playful Great Dane who is already eyeing the agent with grave suspicion.

There was one dog who had been taught – Heaven knows why – to pick up the telephone when it rang and to bark at it. Anyone who has been in an estate agent's office on a busy Saturday morning knows that telephones ring incessantly. This dog – almost a labrador – seemed to resent others answering the phone and ran from desk to desk adopting a most aggressive attitude towards anyone who raised the handset first. It took a long time for the office to recover from that; and the full effects of the barking response on vendors and applicants alike on the other end of the line have never been properly calculated.

Meanwhile, the children are still at large. Bowls of paperclips, mugs with pencils in them and the contents of the wastepaper bins are instinctive targets for little fingers. Those

three targets merge surprisingly quickly and spread across floor and furniture at an extraordinary rate. Wise agents have now produced a range of toys, very large sweets (they reduce the noise levels), colouring books and other devices just to protect the paper-clips, the pencils, the waste-bins and their own sanity.

It is interesting to consider that some applicants will be ready to divulge all to their bank and building society managers, but not to the estate agents. It may be something to do with the estate agents' image – untrustworthy, sharp, making easy money. We now know that this is not true: the estate agent is hard-working, upright and there only to help vendor and applicant alike. Nowadays, of course, the estate agent might work under the banner of a bank, an insurance company or a building society. This phenomenon is relatively recent and is an important part of the history of agency.

6 INTERLUDE – THE BIG LEAGUE

Estate agents are, by their nature, determined individualists. They have a predisposition to hard work, are prepared for the unsocial hours their chosen job demands and can swallow the disappointments and frustrations it may bring. Most estate agencies started as one-man bands, one man with entrepreneurial flair. Those men (and you won't forget that women are included in that term, will you?) were, in most cases, concerned to provide a good service and to survive in a highly competitive market.

As has already been explained, modern agency has an ancestry which was quite respectable, at least as respectable as some of the other trades and professions which are still with us. Agency, for one reason or another, developed a rotten image; it was probably due, more than anything else, to those exceptional occasions when the vendor instructed an agent who just happened to have an eager applicant on the telephone. Within twenty minutes, the applicant would be round to view the house and make an offer. Although that doesn't happen very often, particularly in less buoyant times, the cry of outrage from the vendor when he receives the invoice at the standard rate is so loud that it reaches the national press. If there is nothing else to write about on the day, the story receives the full 'shock, horror' treatment and becomes a talking point in pubs, working men's clubs and elegant dinner parties throughout the country. It is that money for old rope syndrome which we were talking about earlier.

To earn that money for old rope, our entrepreneurial agent had to have properties to sell and applicants to buy them. He therefore had to have premises with a telephone, a typewriter and either a duplicator or a copying machine. His premises could be that front parlour or, if he had enough money, a side-street shop in which he could sit and to which the world could beat a path. Nothing very plush, and the capital investment would be kept to an absolute minimum.

Good and ambitious estate agents, however, wanted to be where people could see them. They therefore sought what are known as prime pitches for their offices: beside major stores in the High Street would do very nicely, thank you. House buyers need money and the building societies were quick to realise that estate agents with a prime pitch were excellent cash receiving points for their savers and, what is more, cheap advertising windows. Closer relationships developed and the agents had agreements with building societies for block allocations of money. While all of this was going on, the usual stream of abuse was being hurled at estate agents and the examples of high fees for apparently no work were being bandied about, whether they were true or false. This was, in fact a confidence trick in reverse. The agents themselves knew better. To earn a crust, agents knew that they had to work very hard indeed and, if they appeared sharp, it was only because they had to take advantage of every opportunity. Their protests went unheeded: the consumer protection people, the script writers and, later, banks, building societies and insurance companies, would not be persuaded that agency was anything but easy money. Anybody, but anybody, they said, could be an estate agent – which was perfectly true if the people concerned had the stamina, the stomach and the wit for it.

The banks, the building societies and the insurance companies – all, you will notice, in a position to offer financial services to house buyers – began to assess what the estate agencies had which they hadn't. The agents had properties for sale and sometimes long lists of applicants aching to buy them. Each vendor was a potential buyer somewhere else. If he was buying up, he would need help. If he was buying down, because of retirement or just plain thrift, he would have surplus cash to invest in pension plans, endowment policies or equities. As for the applicants, they were fair game for all kinds of financial services which would bring profit and a rosy glow to boardroom faces. The agents also had shop windows in busy places.

What began modestly as acquisitions by the famous trotting bank which started the run developed into a frantic race. The race had started in boom times when agents had so many applicants that they were falling over each other for selling instructions. People were buying up, buying down, buying in all directions – and the pace of acquisition was fired by the record lending by the financial institutions. Insurance companies and building societies particularly saw the prospect of enormous profits. Because they were numerate and could themselves borrow fairly cheaply, they did their sums and their forecasts, got them wrong and, in consequence, were prepared to offer large sums of money for going agency concerns – even if some of the agencies weren't going as fast as they should or could.

The agents on whom these riches fell thought that it was perpetual Christmas. Some larger outlets were bought for hundreds of thousands of pounds. Some insurance companies spent tens of millions of pounds on building up estate agency chains, not quite overnight, but remarkably quickly. And then boom turned to bust: the housing market collapsed, first and worst in the prosperous south-east where a high proportion of the new big 'institutional' chains was based. The prospect of profit turned into the reality of loss – not just a few thousand pounds here and there, but tens of millions of pounds belonging, it is fair to suppose, to shareholders who were mostly little people paying premiums. One estate agent who had sold his little chain for a million or two at the peak of institutional desire has just bought it back for a song, now that the ardour has cooled and realism has overtaken passion. How did you become really rich, Grandad? Well, I had these estate agencies, didn't I, way back in 1984 . . .

What went wrong? The market collapse didn't help; but the real reason is deeper than that. After all, market collapse or not, the smaller one, two or three branch agencies have survived it. They have trimmed their sails, perhaps, and developed a leaner, hungrier look; but they have survived. Why? Because they were, above all else – estate agents. They knew – and still know – that agency is about people and caring, about working late and getting up early on Sunday morning to do an accompanied viewing, or just driving around the patch to see what the competition is up to; and making sure that the competition doesn't steal a march on you by cutting fees or offering a free dishwasher with every sale.

Some of the big-league institutional buyers have abandoned their agency ambitions altogether after incurring sensational losses. Others have stuck at it, admitting that they too have incurred sensational losses, but forecasting, hoping, even praying, that all will come right in the end. They will have learned a few expensive lessons. They will have learned, most of all, that successful agency is not as easy as it looks.

The Prudential it was which made the largest and most expensive gaffe. The Pru's entry into the estate agency world probably cost in excess of £200 million, but it might have been £300 million or even £500 million. The sums are a bit difficult to do, because I become easily confused after three noughts. In 1985 or thereabouts, the major insurance companies were stuffed to the gills with money. As has been said, many of them began to look longingly at estate agency as a medium for selling their financial services; and, it has to be said again, as a medium for easy profits. The house market was booming; both sales and prices were going through the roof. It all looked so easy. The Pru began to buy estate agencies – not just one here and there, but whole chains. When you buy in boom conditions, values are high. A.C. Frost, a thirty-shop agency chain in London and the Home Counties, was bought at roughly £500,000 a shop. That is big money to start with, but the spending did not stop there: central management decided to 'brand' each branch with the Pru image – that rather winsome girl wearing a kind of bandanna in grey and an off-red colour.

Now we've all heard about the cost of changing an image. None of us who is a shareholder in British Telecom has quite recovered from the shift from what we had just about begun to recognise at roughly the same time that we stopped calling it the Post Office. They, if you remember, suddenly introduced that spritely fellow with a flute or a yard of ale – but what really had the impact was the cost. Most people just don't believe what it is alleged to have cost – again I am confused about all those noughts – but it is not difficult to imagine. All those forms, vehicle liveries – it just doesn't bear thinking about.

And so it was with the Pru. Facias, 'For Sale' boards, stationery – you might think that they would be expensive enough, but they also changed the carpets, the furniture and the computers. They made the female staff wear uniforms and the male staff wear Prudential-type ties. This was happening not just in the thirty or so branches bought from A.C. Frost, but in all the branches which the Pru bought – and there were hundreds. Worse, the Pru overlooked the fact that agency, as readers will now be aware, is a local, caring, hard-working business: decisions were made centrally, writ in tablets of stone and passed down to the branch managers to implement. Competitive freedom was lost, which didn't matter as much in the early days as it did later when boom turned to bust. By September 1989, the Pru had closed two hundred of its branches. About one thousand members of staff – an unhappy mix of managers, negotiators and typists – had been made redundant. By January 1991, the Pru had withdrawn totally from estate agency. The branches that they had bought for many millions of pounds were sold, often to the very people from whom they had been acquired, at a fraction of the original purchase price. There are many happy people around, but not, I suspect, in the Prudential boardroom.

Others can, of course, learn from this expensive adventure, although we know, don't we, that agency is not easy. Agency is essentially a local activity. Managers and staff of agency outlets must know their patch, their pricing and their local economics. Some remote personnel officer is not the person to play Monday morning chess with staff when a manager goes sick or a negotiator fails to turn up. The surviving big chains, and there are several, are unlikely to make the same mistakes as the Pru. Not now, anyway; local management, giving local service and with a freedom to compete, is recognised as the vital estate agency ingredient.

Competition there is aplenty. When the big chains were being developed through wholesale acquisition, there was just a hint that estate agencies were being established solely in the hope that a good fairy in the form of an insurance company or building society would pop up and buy them. It actually happened, and there are one or two bright young men living it up in the Costa del Somewhere to prove it. They are still working as estate agents, of course, but they are tanned and much warmer. We already heard that there is no requirement for an estate agent to register before he can practise. He needs no qualifications if he is determined to remain, as he has every right to do, one of the 'unattached'. He does not have to be a member of the RICS, ISVA or the NAEA to be an estate agent. And he can probably get started from his front room with a telephone and a photocopier.

To be fair, the principle of what the Pru was trying to do had great promise. What is known as 'one-stop shopping' has considerable appeal. So far in this narrative, we have concerned ourselves primarily with our friendly local estate agent. There are, however, other players in the drama of house transfer, all of whom will seek to extract fees from the buyer or the seller or both. To the uninitiated, the rush from agent to lawyers to building societies to structural surveyor and then back to lawyer and back to the estate agent is all rather overwhelming. Lurking in the background are the local authorities with their local land charges registers, not to mention HM Land Registry who can lose whole piles of documents at the rattle of a tea cup. All of this is confusing and frustrating, even to those who are supposed to understand the system.

For a buyer to walk into one office where, if it is organised properly, he doesn't even have to move from his chair, has a dreamlike quality about it. Estate agents, lawyers, mortgage managers, insurance agents and surveyors will all be there to do his bidding with a handsome (or beautiful) young negotiator ready to drive him out to his ideal home for an accompanied viewing, even with the kids.

While the big buy-outs were going on, another modest little battle was being fought between solicitors who felt they should have had the monopoly of conveyancing work and the conveyancing companies (akin to those scriveners we were talking about earlier) who felt they shouldn't. However, the conveyancing companies were prepared to carry out the conveyancing work at low cost. The solicitors read the political signs wrongly, because Mrs Thatcher had no taste for monopolies (except in government) and both forms of conveyancing now exist.

There was yet another skirmish going on at about the same time. Others outside the big league were persuaded that estate agency was just a matter of sticking a picture of a house in a window and letting the buying public stare at it for a minute or two before rushing in to buy it. These were shops without agency service. There was no advice on pricing, no accompanied viewing, no knowledge of the worthiness of the potential buyer and, in most cases, it meant money up-front for a month's exposure in a shop window. Again, there is nothing wrong with the principle of what the proprietors were trying to do; it was the vendors who took the risk and paid their money. The risks can be explained by a true example. A dear old widowed lady decided that her large North London house was just too big for her to manage; she was entirely alone and had decided to move herself into a retirement home. Her house had been purchased at a time, probably forty years before, when a mansion could be bought for two thousand pounds. Times had changed and the old lady's house was probably worth £300,000 when she sat there filling in her form, trying to remember how many bedrooms it had. She asked the chap sitting next to her how much he thought her house was worth. He knew the road and the quality of the houses in it simply because he was a local estate agent doing what all estate agents do – checking out the competition. The estate agent gave his opinion: in the region of £300,000 subject to inspection. She thought that sounded rather a lot. The agent tried to reassure her but, eventually, she settled for £200,000, writing the amount in large figures on her form. It is to the credit of the estate agent that he didn't buy it there and then and sell it at its true value.

Another example of someone misunderstanding the basic rules of agency, perhaps? Maybe somebody else believing the hype that house transfer was easy and that the intermediary made a killing without much effort. One of the interesting facts about modern professional people – and we will, for the time being at least, ignore the government's view that agency is a business and not a profession – is that they no longer run on fixed lines. If they see somebody else, some other professional, making money, they want to have a go at it themselves. The principle of 'me too' doesn't only apply to agency. Banks, particularly American ones, have set themselves up as property consultants offering commercial agency and marketing services to all and sundry. Management consultants, almost instinctively, are treading on everyone's patch, and most of their toes. Jobs such as project management and facilities management, largely because they are ill-defined, attract all kinds of hopefuls: architects, surveyors, quantity surveyors, engineers, interior designers, management consultants (of course), they all offer themselves as whizz-kids in these fields. There is a blurring of the edges of professionalism. Only the medical profession seems to remain aloof; after all, not everyone can be a brain surgeon and, certainly, not everyone even wants to try.

In Scotland, the lawyers have always had a place in residential agency. In fact, they have been front runners. Scottish housing law is different from the English variety and the lawyers hold a key position; traditionally, they have handled house sales from start to finish. Lawyers in England saw some of the apparently extortionate fees charged by agents for what seemed to them to be effortless introductions and the 'me too' bug bit deeply. Many lawyers became infected. Again, a few lessons have been learned. Lawyers had variable levels of success and failure, but what they were trying to do was probably right. That principle of one-stop shopping has its merits.

The estate agents themselves are not all that wedded to purity of function. As the big battalions were moving in to buy up some agencies, other agents were creating their own financial services companies, forming their own structural survey teams and either establishing their own conveyancing companies or linking with existing ones. Most estate agents had always had a useful additional income from insurance work anyway, and every effort was made by them to bolster it.

When estate agents abandoned their purity of function and jumped on the bandwagon of financial services, they risked committing the sin of their opposite numbers in financial services who were jumping on theirs! It is difficult to keep a broad sweep of services in watertight compartments. Surveys carried out at the time people were finding their feet in other professionals' jungles showed that members of the house buying and selling public were both confused and upset. 'He seemed keener to sell me an endowment policy and a mortgage than a house' was a frequent comment. One pair of grand-parents, moving down market in price terms and consequently likely to have a cash surplus, found themselves with a school fees plan for the grandchildren when all they had asked for was for their house to be sold.

Estate agents, as we have said, are rugged individualists. They hate being taken for a ride. When local newspapers increased advertising rates drastically some years ago, agents stopped, momentarily at least, being rugged individualists: they got together and became press barons themselves. They published their own newspapers which, although mostly consisting of property advertising, actually contained editorial on house transfer and its problems. Every house, often over wide areas, had its own copy of the newspaper stuffed through its letter box. Design, printing, delivery, indeed the whole production and distribution system was put into place with circulation and readership figures far higher than those of the local newspapers which started the fight in the first place.

So everybody is at it. The public probably has every right to get confused. At the same time, government, in the name of consumer protection, has the right to control some of the excesses of high pressure selling and the provision of misleading information which can slip easily from simple zeal into criminal offence.

7 AND MORE OF THE PROCESS

Despite all the obvious barriers to progress, both real and imagined, we will have to assume, if we are to finish this book, that vendor and buyer actually agree a price. Agreement will usually have been reached through the medium of the estate agent, who ends up feeling like a table tennis ball after a serious professional tournament. Although he is acting for the vendor and is bound to act in the vendor's best interests, the estate agent really wants to sell the place so that he actually earns a fee. This places him in the most difficult of positions; and the only way out is through absolute honesty.

Too many people assume that the agent instinctively forces the vendor's price down and the buyer's price up, no matter how far apart the two figures may be. But our estate agent is a good estate agent: he knows the current market price – give or take a few hundred pounds – and he knows which way the market is going, whether up or down. He knows how busy the market is and what interest he has had in this particular property. More importantly, he knows the strengths and weaknesses of both the potential buyer and the vendor. He is in a position to make very precise judgements. Those judgements are the test of the agent's integrity.

There is a basic assumption that the agent doesn't have any – integrity, that is. But any aspiring agent, whether he has integrity or not, should consider the consequences of seeking to clinch a deal, come what may, at everybody's expense but his own. A reputation for being pushy gets around. It is surprising that it does; after all, buyers and sellers are individuals, they belong to no group or association of buyers and sellers. They do not, so far as I have been able to trace, have a club headquarters; nor do they arrange mass rallies in Trafalgar Square. But, despite all this, what they feel about estate agents, both in general and in particular, gets around: 'Well, he said we just wouldn't sell it if we didn't knock £3,000 off the price' or 'He told us that fourteen other people were after it and all of them had offered more than we had'. There is no literal expression of mistrust in these words but, if they are used too often, labels begin to be attached to particular firms and individuals.

Valuation is an imprecise art. It is said that the true value of a building is what a willing buyer will pay to a willing seller, but when it comes to buying and selling houses, we are all like stall-holders in an Arab souk. It is all to do with urgency and timing; about financial strengths and weaknesses; about what else is available and how many 'real' buyers there are. The wise agent advises both sides honestly and leaves the decision-making to buyer and seller. He is allowed to keep his fingers crossed.

Any offer by a buyer, if the buyer is well advised, will be subject to contract and satisfactory structural survey. Neither party – and we are talking about England and Wales – is bound by the making and acceptance of an offer expressed in this way. The words can, however, lead to all kinds of may-hem – while the agent, who has only uncrossed his fingers long enough to bite his nails, frets in his office wondering whether he will get his fee.

There are two kinds of survey. The first is demanded by the funding source; although the luckless buyer pays for it, as often as not the funding source would rather he didn't see it. There was a time when funders agreed between themselves that no buyer should be allowed within sight of the survey report, but in these more competitive days some building societies have loosened their stays just a little. What is known as the building society survey or valuation is, anyway, of little reassurance to the buyer. The valuer is asked to express his view of value in the event of forced sale in the open market. In addition, without carrying out a full structural survey, the valuer will draw attention to the more obvious defects such as the absence of a roof or the theft of all the fittings from the bathroom. He may recommend the retention of a proportion of any advance until specific defects are remedied.

You will understand our agent's nerve-twitching concern. If the value is too low, the offer from the funding source will also be low – perhaps too low to permit the buyer to proceed. If the valuer has pointed to obvious defects and suggested a retention of part of an advance until they are dealt with, the buyer could well try to bring the price down to match. On the other hand, he might just get fed-up with the whole business and become a gypsy. Neither course is good for our agent's morale.

It is, however, nothing compared with what could happen as a result of a fully-fledged structural survey by a real expert in building construction and the ailments to which buildings can succumb. It is in the interests of the buyer to have a structural survey undertaken by a qualified professional. Let there be no doubt about that: there is a Latin tag – *caveat emptor* – which means 'buyer beware' or 'don't be a sucker', depending on which school you went to.

There is quite a lot one can say about structural surveys and structural surveyors. The true professionals spent years learning about soffits*, architraves, wet rot, dry rot and several species of wood-boring beetles. When you have spent years learning about something, you tend to want to be sure that everyone knows just how clever you are. So the report, even when the building is given a clean bill of health, is full of words that nobody who hasn't had the same years of specialist training actually understands. The reports are also usually long because the surveyor (although he might just as well be an architect or an engineer) hasn't the time to write a short one which would be clear to a fourteen year old with a reading age of eight; because that is what is needed, particularly if the building is fit. Often, the way these reports are expressed, the dazed buyer is convinced by round about page 12 that the place will collapse on his wife, children and dog while he is away at the office. If the building has anything wrong with it, the details of its sickness will read like the more extreme paragraphs of Edgar Allan Poe and have the potential buyer reading catalogues for easy-to-erect tents.

It is wise to repeat the advice that it is in the buyer's best interests to have a full structural survey carried out. The problem, quite apart from those already listed, is that the buyer has to pay for it. Structural surveys are often expensive. If a buyer is unlucky and has been pipped at the post on two or three houses, he might spend his hard-earned money on two or three structural surveys. There have been suggestions that the vendor should pay for the structural survey and give a copy to every applicant or, if the photocopying of a 40-page report is too hard on the pocket, a copy could be made available to be read in the agent's office. Or, and this would be ideal, every house should have its own log book: a record of condition, repairs, maintenance and improvements. Even that would not take into account the harm that can be done to the fabric of a building by the do-it-yourself enthusiast.

The professionals who carry out full structural surveys usually have 'professional indemnity insurance'. This protects the users of their services from the financial effects of professional negligence or those little acts of human frailty like not noticing the wormholes in the staircase. But even the most careful professionals, surrounded by insurance policies, cannot get it right all the time. Many years ago, there was a small bungalow estate on the fringe of an Essex town; most of the estate is still there. Essex has, in parts, an unhappy mixture of clay and running sand. One day a bungalow sank and none of the experts called in to examine the phenomenon could have predicted the event. It just happened, after years of the bungalow just sitting there being a bungalow. The distraught owners even dragged the original builder from his stool in the local pub, but he could show that he had taken trial holes before putting in the foundations. An expert local authority building inspectorate had watched the construction carefully – they knew about running sand – but could find no fault. The structural survey carried out when the bungalow changed hands was professionally competent. No one knew that, because of some distant deeper excavation, the sand that was keeping the bungalow up was running away, slowly but surely. Just think, it could be happening to you this very minute. Ownership has its responsibilities.

Our estate agent, through long and tiresome experience of structural surveys, will, by now, have bitten his nails down to his knuckles. He can imagine what is going through his buyer's mind as he reads about soffits*, architraves, wet rot, dry rot and the ravages of wood-boring beetles. He knows that there is a 70:30 chance that his buyer will get cold feet, even before the bungalow sinks.

In some respects, our agent must rely on the wisdom of the buyer's lawyer. When the agent has brought seller and buyer together, when they have finally agreed a price and a deal has been struck, subject to contract and structural survey, our agent has one or two things to do. It may be that the buyer will require a loan on the security of the house he is buying. Funding of house purchase is a fairly complicated subject and deserves a chapter all to itself. But the agent is often in a position to help; he may have a strong relationship with a building society, perhaps with two or three. He will set the funding ball rolling. Indeed, he may have kicked the ball off the centre spot a long time ago and you will remember that, by friendly but persistent interrogation in the face of awful hardship, he has extracted from his buyer all he needs to know about that poor soul's financial position. But let us get back to the wisdom of the buyer's lawyer.

As soon as the deal is struck, the agent writes to the lawyers for both sides informing them of the arrangements. Everything that the lawyers want to know and which can reasonably be provided by the agent is conveyed in these letters. The buyer's lawyer, wise and accustomed to the language of structural surveys, can guide his client through the report and help him to make a decision. This is, quite properly, the buyer's lawyer's job. The agent, you will remember, is acting for the vendor. It would be difficult for him to run counter to *his* client's interests by telling the buyer to withdraw because of the bowing of the front wall or a sagging soffit (whatever it is that soffits actually do)*.

There are some parts of the country where mining causes subsidence which has damaged houses. There are some houses in the country which are built in such a way that their life is limited, through what are now recognised as defective materials or insecure design. Some houses, through lack of care and maintenance, have fallen into such a derelict condition that the best hope for their future is demolition and replacement. After reading a structural surveyor's report, whatever the true condition of the house, the nervous buyer is firmly of the belief that the place is like all the examples I have given and is in danger of imminent collapse. He needs reassurance; and the person to give it is his own lawyer.

Another feature of this nail-biting period before contracts are exchanged is now known as gazumping. This is a good old Yiddish word which was much in use in the busy markets of the East End of London before they became bazaars and were taken over by other races. The original word was *gazumph*, meaning to swindle, but its application to the world of estate agency came much later. In that context, it means that another potential buyer increases his bid to secure the house of his dreams when the first buyer has already shaken hands with the vendor and agreed a price. Gazumping is at its most severe when house sales are buoyant, the building societies are lending liberally and there is a shortage of houses for sale. Buoyancy, liberal lending and shortage are the recipe for boom and the ingredients of gazumping. When gazumping was common during the booms in house sales, estate agents took most of the blame. Buyers who had been gazumped felt that they had been let down by their agents. This was unfair because, you will remember, the agent acts for the vendor and it is his duty to convey to the vendor all the offers he receives. Although the agent, because of his knowledge of the strengths and weaknesses of the potential buyers, will advise the vendor, it is the vendor who makes the decision as to whom he will sell. The problem is compounded when multiple-agency instructions have been given by the vendor. All of the instructed agents have the ambition to steal a march on their competitors and are usually willing to encourage *their* potential buyers to add a few hundred pounds to the price, because that means a fat fee for the successful agent and gloom and despondency for the rest.

When the market is really hot, gazumpers can themselves be gazumped. In fact, keenness to acquire is at the roots of rapid price escalation. It is called demand in a free market. Deals done at the higher prices are then regarded as 'market indicators' and, for the next round of sales of similar houses, the higher price becomes the base price with a few hundred pounds or even a few thousand pounds added for luck. Even in less buoyant times, gazumping can happen. We have already seen how one feature – however uninspiring it may appear to others – can appeal to a buyer and, more particularly, to a buyer's wife. You will remember the stained glass window in East London. If a potential buyer sets his heart on a particular property, if only to sustain domestic harmony, he might be prepared to spend just a little more to acquire it; and then a little more, and then a little more, up to the point at which he can no longer afford it.

When something deeply desired is lost, the disappointment and frustration create anger. That anger is usually directed towards the person who breaks the bad news, in our case, the estate agent. You can be sure that the vendor will leave all the unpleasantness to the agent. After all, why shouldn't he? He is paying the bill at the end of the day. That is why the agents attracted much of the odium when gazumping was a daily occurrence in dozens – no, thousands – of cases throughout the country. Some agents, being sensitive souls, tried hard to be fair not only to their vendors, but also to the applicants who, as keen potential buyers, were prepared to bid ever upwards. Often, the agent would call the competing buyers into his office. Everyone would sit round a table with the inevitable cup of coffee. The agent would explain that a halt had to be called to the spiral and that the purpose of the meeting was to conclude a deal on which neither vendor nor buyer would renege. One agent issued scraps of paper to the bidders and asked them to write down their name and price. He would then collect the scraps of paper and announce, not the winner, but that he had a price of so many thousands, without naming who had made it. He would then issue more scraps of paper, repeating the procedure as long as competition continued. Some bidders would fall out as the price became too fierce for them, probably leaving in a huff after the first round. Eventually, someone would emerge as the highest bidder.

Some potential buyers, faced with this kind of nerve-racking experience, believed that it was simply a device by the agent to force up the price to unrealistic levels. In some cases, of course, this was the effect. Occasionally, an unlucky buyer, who knew that it was his price which was quoted by the agent as the highest in the first round of bids, added another £2,000 to his figure just to be sure that he would secure the house, only to find that all the other bidders had dropped out. Quite naturally, he was, to say the least, annoyed. He had just spent £2,000 for no reason whatsoever.

Other agents merely telephoned all the buyers, told them that there were three or four bidders forcing up the price and inviting them to deliver sealed bids to the agent at his office before a specified time for opening. This seemed a fair way to proceed and was widely practised, mostly following the suggestion of the agent who, of course, had to carry the vendor along with him. But, whichever way finality was reached, it was the vendor who made the last and nearly binding decision – subject, of course, to contract and structural survey. It was, as we have said, the agent who collected the criticism and faced the anger of the unsuccessful bidders – sometimes even the criticism and anger of the winner who believed he had been taken for a ride.

The buoyancy of the market when gazumping became almost the norm resulted in an unprecedented rise in house prices. Vendors, it has to be said, became plain greedy. Agents who had detected the first signs of a coming collapse in the house market tried hard to persuade vendors that they were asking too much – and some of the quoted falls in house prices were, in a sense, unreal, because the fall had been calculated from a height that was never actually achieved. Recent reports of millions of pounds being carved off the prices of top houses and estates, even newly built penthouses, show that vendors were really piling it on, whatever the advice from their agents happened to be.

Although cases of gazumping have been cited in Scotland, the practice is much less prevalent there than in the rest of the country. Scottish law makes gazumping difficult, although apparently not impossible. However, once a vendor and buyer have agreed a price, the potential gazumper can only gnash his teeth. A canny lot, the Scots – and why the rest of us don't do it that way is difficult to understand.

So let us return to our relatively straightforward case in a less than buoyant market. The vendor and buyer have agreed a price, subject to contract and to structural survey. The estate agent has informed the solicitors for both sides of the transaction and, if necessary, has sent the applicant off to a building society to apply for a loan. The estate agent may have a close relationship with a building society, indeed, he may be owned by one. For our purposes, we will assume that our estate agent is an independent. He may have access to funds of several building societies and he will know, because he keeps closely in touch with them, who is lending the most and on what terms. He has, as we all now know to the point of boredom, extracted every scrap of information from the applicant about his financial status. It is in the agent's interest to help the applicant towards an adequate loan, because that is also in the vendor's interests and it is the vendor who pays the agent's fee. And that always was, so far as the agent is concerned, the point of the exercise.

What the agent has done up to now has been entirely proper. It may be that, if he can persuade the buyer to secure his building society advance with an endowment policy, he will attract a bit of extra commission which will help to keep the wolf from the door, put a spot of jam on the bread or even create fantasies about that holiday in Bermuda. This is not improper. Taking as many commissions as possible from all and sundry is part of the agent's life. It will have occurred to you that the agent has done an enormous amount of work for the applicant who pays nothing so, if he can make something out of the applicant by way of commission from others, it would be churlish to criticise. After all, there is still a long way to go and, although a deal has been struck, it is pregnant with risk. And the abort rate is high.

One of the reasons for the risk of a sale becoming abortive is what is called 'the chain'. You will remember that our friendly local estate agent expressed delight at the arrival of a first-time buyer, a husband and wife team of high earners in reasonably secure jobs and with no wish to add too quickly to the world's population problems. It is clear that not everyone can be a first-time buyer with no handicap of a house to sell in a poor market. People are buying up, buying down and moving about for a hundred and one reasons. They are doing these things not only in our friendly local agent's patch, but also in Cleethorpes, Wick and Diss. The country is now mobile, quite unlike the days when the ingredients of modern estate agency were being cobbled together by the butcher, baker and undertaker. Our vendor is buying a bigger house somewhere else. The vendor from whom he is buying is buying somewhere else; and so it goes on. Sometimes related chains of sales and purchases can consist of a dozen deals, even more. Each one is subject to risk and, if one sale collapses, there is a chance that the whole chain will disintegrate.

If the chain is confined to our agent's own patch and all the vendors and buyers are negotiating through him, there is just a chance that he will hold the chain together, slipping in a new applicant if one falters or even slipping in a similar property if one has failed to pass the scrutiny of the beady-eyed structural surveyor. But chains are rarely like this; chains actually do consist, too often, of buyers and sellers in places such as Cleethorpes, Wick and Diss. All the buyers and sellers have widely different reasons for moving and widely different degrees of priority or urgency. All are being served by agents of variable levels of efficiency, experience and ability. The agents, naturally, are deeply suspicious of each other in case one should try to steal another's client or applicant. Chains are therefore vulnerable.

Our friendly local estate agent, you will probably agree, has every right to become fretful, even petulant. Here we are attempting to simplify our explanation of the process and we are already in a mess. The agent might have, in a modest little office, a staff of four or five, including Myrtle who still can't stick photographs on straight and is quite unable to grasp the high-technology of the photocopier. He might have a dozen, even twenty, of these transactions going on at the same time. All of them might be in chains of variable lengths and distances apart and all will be at slightly different stages.

As if the system itself wasn't bad enough, things happen to people which cause them to change their minds. There are the obvious things such as unexpected redundancy, bankruptcy or even the death of a spouse. These are serious and perfectly understandable reasons for withdrawal. People withdraw from deals for other reasons, too: 'My wife feels the cat won't like the new place' or 'It doesn't have a Sainsburys'. After a year or two of this kind of thing, exasperation comes easily to an exhausted, twitching agent. And that is even before the lawyers for both sides become involved in the nitty-gritty of house transfer.

Before we get to the lawyers – and we shall have quite enough time with them, believe me – some of you may be thinking that an agent with a staff of three or four, with even a dozen transactions on the go at one time, is absolutely raking it in. Let us examine the facts: he has a prime pitch in the High Street; his rent could, quite easily, be £40,000 a year, plus uniform business rate and the normal overheads associated with the occupation of business property; his property outgoings could easily reach £60,000. Salaries for the staff, and we will assume that he is parsimonious, will be, for five people of various levels, including NIC and all those other things that we call staff benefits, about £75,000. His telephone and postal bills are astronomical and, in an office really fighting for business, the combined total could easily reach £15,000. And then there are the cars: the leasing and running costs for two modest cars might also be about £15,000. Advertising can absorb £1,000 a week so that is another £50,000 a year, assuming a few days off for Christmas. Then there are the 'For Sale boards', and all those mini-prints for Myrtle to play with, the large sweets to keep the kids quiet, the oceans of coffee poured down the throats of callers – well, the list goes on. The cost of running a modest office could reach £250,000 a year.

Assuming, in a tight market, that the agent is working on one and a half per cent and the average house price is £60,000, the commission he earns per house is £900. Bear in mind that the percentage commission figure and the average house price could be substantially lower in some areas, but then, so will the outgoings. Our agent will have to sell 5.34 houses per week to meet his outgoings and he hasn't paid himself a penny so far. Some parts of the year are so quiet in house-buying terms that the agent is likely to be convinced that the country has closed down. Allowing for those periods, it is vital to sell at least seven in a good week – and nine if the agent wants some take-home pay.

You will remember our little diversion into the Pru's brief and expensive flirtation with estate agency. In 1988, because of the downturn and the extraordinary failure of those in charge to recognise that agency is a local, caring business, the Pru branches were selling fewer than two houses a week on average. If you bear in mind the original purchase prices of those hundreds of branches and the money lavished on them and then calculate the loss of interest created by diverting cherished capital into other people's pockets as opposed to investment, two houses a week just weren't enough. Indeed, according to our sums, they were hardly enough to pay the milk bill; and things, as the downturn worsened in the housing market, went from bad to catastrophic. The Pru's average of two sales a week in 1988 for every branch in the network produced total sales of something over 88,000 properties.

You might think that is quite good. After all, if the average commission produces somewhere between £1,000 and £2,000 per sale, we are talking about an income of £100 million, perhaps more. But that was less than the outgoings, if we take into account what was paid for the branches in the first place. Worse, in 1989, the sales figures slipped to less than 40,000. They should have insured against disaster, just as people insure against rain storms on the day of the village fête.

So, our local estate agent, reading his horror comics about how the mighty have fallen, knows that he must sell rather more than two houses a week if he wants to survive. Because he is experienced and wise, he will aim for nine or ten and be grateful for six.

And also bear in mind the abort rate – all those vulnerable chains and the vagaries of the mind-changing public. To be sure of nine sales in a week, and assuming a 70 per cent abort rate, which is not uncommon, our agent should aim for thirty deals which are reasonably healthy before the structural surveyors, building societies and the lawyers get their hands on them.

So let's get our hands on the lawyers.

---

*Just in case you are worried about it, a soffit is the under horizontal face of an architrave or overhanging cornice; the under surface of a lintel, vault, or arch; a ceiling.

8 THE FULL PROCESS OF THE LAW

It seems a fairly straightforward matter to prepare a contract for the sale of a house. In fact, there is a standard form for it and the amount of typing required to fill in the blank spaces is hardly demanding. However, before the lawyer for the buyer allows his client to sign anything at all, he will make 'enquiries before contract'. There is a whole mix of things he has to know to protect the best interests of his client.

Although, as we know, our estate agent is diligent, his detailed particulars of sale are unlikely to have picked up everything about the house that the lawyer will want to know. What covenants exist which would affect his client's full and free enjoyment of the property? Who – and he hopes it isn't his client – is responsible for the maintenance of that rather tatty fence at the bottom of the garden? Where, if it exists at all, is the ten-year guarantee from the woodworm people following the treatment which the vendor paid for five years ago?

These 'enquiries before contract' are addressed by the buyer's solicitor to the vendor's solicitor who, at this stage of the game, has no idea of the answers either. The vendor's solicitor will have received our local estate agent's letter informing him of the deal. As our local estate agent has gone out of his way to be helpful, he might have given the vendor's lawyer a note of existing mortgage arrangements and the name of the society; it is possible, but unlikely. So the vendor's solicitor could have started his particular ball rolling by asking the vendor for the deeds or the whereabouts of the deeds. If he had acted for the vendor when he acquired the property all those years ago, he will have a file for it; but he has to find it. If the sale was the average of seven years ago, finding it will be hard enough. If it was fifteen or twenty years ago, well, anything might have happened to it.

There was once a private garage beside the offices of a highly respected firm of solicitors, which the highly respected firm used for the storage of deeds. When the private garage was first hired, it was fitted out with shelving and then the deeds and their supporting documentation were put in packets, tied with pink tape and everything was labelled. It was really very efficient. And then, one day, a disaffected member of staff went berserk and emptied the contents of every packet on to the floor. The place was knee-deep in deeds and supporting documentation. The chances of finding anything ever again depended almost entirely on luck; there was not much of that.

Some lawyers' offices are like that even without a demented member of staff creating the chaos in the first place. Filing chaos creeps up on lawyers in the night, which is filled with evil gremlins slipping the documents about one transaction into the file about another. Lawyers, of course, have more papers than newsagents and the sheer volume and weight of acres of ex-forests scudding about their offices would make David Bellamy suffer severe trauma.

It is said that lawyers can find a valid objection to every possible solution. All their training and all the case law that they stuff into their heads – not to mention Rumpole of the Bailey on the telly – fits them for litigation and confrontation. If there is something wrong, some weakness in what the 'opposition' is offering, the chances are that they will sniff it out. There is a great risk that legal ping-pong will exasperate everybody – the vendor, the buyer and, of course, the estate agent whose knuckles are now down to his elbows.

When we were going on about the early history of estate agency, we mentioned the surveyors – the overseers of those landed estates – who developed the skill of preparing plans of what they oversaw on behalf of their patrons. We might have given the impression that they were really rather good at drawing plans. Certainly, their pure land surveying descendants who are now responsible for the sheer perfection of the Ordnance Survey in this country can be relied upon to produce accurate plans of the bits of land on which our vendor's house is built. Unfortunately, those pure land surveying descendants will have had no hand in the preparation of the plans attached to the deeds with which we are now concerned. They are likely to have been drawn by the descendant of someone or something quite different – probably one of those artistically-inclined chimpanzees who splash colour on board in a creative frenzy. Deed plans, for reasons which are not easy to understand, show boundaries drawn with a one inch brush so that precise boundary definition is impossible. Lines are so thick that they cover completely streams, hedgerows and those little 'T' marks which indicate fencing responsibilities. They are usually devoid of a north point, which doesn't usually matter all that much, although that particular omission has caused occasional disaster on green fields sites.

The deeds themselves, of course, are silent on the very points on which the buyer's lawyer will want to make his enquiries before contract. If the last conveyance is, say, fifty years old, there will be a reference to 'as delineated on the plan annexed hereto'. The plan annexed hereto shows absolutely nothing with any accuracy. If the deeds refer to dimensions at all, they will say of a frontage 'so many feet or thereabouts'. The 'thereabouts' is critical because it is the 'thereabouts' which causes friction between neighbours – particularly if a tree growing on the 'thereabouts' becomes dangerous and has to be felled or lopped at enormous expense. The consequence of this is that the vendor's lawyers build into their answers to the enquiries before contract a thickness of armour normally reserved for Chieftain tanks. 'Not so far as I am aware' is a favourite and, in the circumstances, reasonably reassuring. 'We have no information on this point' introduces the first niggling doubt and 'refer to the local authority' brings on a cloud of uncertainty.

Local authorities are bound to maintain what is known as the Register of Local Land Charges. Local land charges have nothing to do with the Council Tax, the Poll Tax, the Uniform Business Rate or any other fiscal device which central or local government chooses to impose on its unfortunate residents. They are charges on land (and land always includes buildings, of course) which impose some sort of duty or responsibility on the owner, such as combined drainage orders. If a group of houses is close to the main sewer, the cheapest way to connect all the houses to that sewer is to run a new pipe along the back or front of them and connect the individual houses to that new pipe which then runs into the main sewer. The local authority won't adopt the new pipe or the individual connections to it. Their responsibility stops – or I suppose that really should be starts – at the main sewer. The local authority makes a Combined Drainage Order. If the local authority actually does the work initially of digging all the trenches, laying the pipes, making the connections and then filling everything in again, there might be a cost to be repaid by the owners. Until the debt is paid off, there is a charge on the individual buildings. But it goes on, because the Order provides for joint responsibility for future care and maintenance. That is a local land charge – and there are dozens of things that can affect a building or a piece of land which must go into the Register of Local Land Charges.

Few local authorities can reasonably be described as cavalier; well, perhaps some of them might be, but such is the weight of legislation round their necks, such is the frequency of public complaint, that they don't remain cavalier for long. But whether it is administrative pressure such as someone calling a general election which brings unexpected work loadings, or just plain forgetfulness, it is difficult to say, some things just don't get registered. Some local authorities might, therefore, be thought to be cavalier in respect of their registration duties. Local authorities are like that. Under the Civil Defence Act of 1948, local authorities were required to make arrangements for the defence of the civil population in the event of war – wardens, rescue sections, whistles, steel helmets, stirrup pumps – all the paraphernalia of the 1939-45 fracas which we threw away when the all-clear sounded. Some local authorities took it all very seriously and brought new arrangements into force quickly and efficiently to meet the requirements of the Act. Some achieved success almost by accident largely because all the old wardens, rescue sections, ambulance drivers and so on had so missed the camaraderie of the war years that they wanted an excuse to renew old friendships and to go to the pub for a drink together again. And what did other local authorities do? Declare nuclear-free zones! So much for duty.

That may have little relevance to local land charges, but take the case of the Public Health Acts, which are much nearer to home. Local authorities were required to maintain a sewer map: when you lay pipes of different dimensions all over the place, it is a good idea to know where you have put them. A very reasonable requirement, you might think. Some local authorities didn't get around to preparing their sewer maps all that quickly and, anyway, in the major conurbations, there were already dozens of pipes which had been laid long before the Act imposed the duty. Even the Romans were at it in an odd kind of way. After building licensing was brought to an end in 1956 and the country woke up to the fact that house building should be a priority, people wanted to know where the sewers actually were. Twenty years after the passing of the Act, some local authorities just didn't know. They knew where some of them were, of course, but *all* of them – well, no, that was when Mr Bloggs was engineer and surveyor and no one had told him about the Act.

The chief executive of one local authority at the time discovered, to his ill-concealed delight, that a depot foreman had the gift of divining. Sewers contain what passes for water

and, when an enquiry was received from some developer anxious to drive his piles into a virgin piece of land, Bert would emerge from his depot with his willow wand and pinpoint to the inch the location, line and depth of the sewer. Bert would then appear at the office with a grubby piece of paper on which he had drawn the line of the sewer (with depth indications) and this priceless information was then plotted on what had become the sewer map. Bert didn't always have the time to walk the whole length of the sewer on every occasion that his skills were brought into play so the sewer map showed lines that started in the middle of one field, went purposefully along for about two inches (at five inches to the mile) and then stopped in the middle of another field. If that particular sewer map were to be placed in a time capsule, it would baffle its discoverer in 2192.

If we bear this kind of thing in mind, it is reasonable to suppose that the buyer's lawyer does not always have a great deal of confidence in the results of his written search in the Register of Local Land Charges. It is, nevertheless, part of the procedure which he must follow. But that is not all: in addition to the charges which must be registered because of some statutory whim, there is a mass of other information lurking in the local authority's gift which is of great value to a lawyer dutifully guarding his buyer client's interests. Most lawyers will tell you that the answers to the supplementary enquiries are – or should be – of much greater value than what is normally contained in the Register of Local Land Charges. The problem is that this valuable information is likely to be spread across a dozen departments of the local authority.

The borough surveyor will have some of it; the environmental health officer will have some of it; the housing officer might have a smidgeon. The medical officer of health might well have a point of view about something, but not often. When a requisition for a search is received with its attendant list of supplementary enquiries, the local land charges clerk becomes like a demented ant running hither and fro to draw together all this information. If there are a large number of transactions going on at the same time, dementia increases in proportion. The busy engineers, environmental health officers, medical officers of health and housing officers, even the planning officers who are an essential part of the process, will all have much more important things to do than worry about a demented ant. Consider for a moment that, in boom times, the said demented ant can have as many as one hundred requisitions for official search with all the supplementary enquiries stacked high on his desk. Although the lawyers will, indeed must, pay a fee for the privilege of the search – which they will later charge on to the buyer client – local authorities do not generally regard responses to requisitions as a significant priority. Some take as long as ten weeks to respond. There is no entry in the *Guinness Book of Records*, but the longest period of silence is thought to be in excess of sixteen weeks – although, with what people are saying about local authorities these days, that record could have been smashed a dozen times.

Quite apart from the effects of delay on our vulnerable deal (remember gazumping and those awful chains) the deepening effect on the emotions and sanity of our estate agent is awful to behold. The lawyer can, of course, if he wishes, make a personal search just to speed up the process. The average local land charges clerk, faced with an angry and impatient lawyer at the reception hatch demanding the privilege of a personal search, suffers even more than our estate agent. A personal search will disclose the weaknesses of the system. If the lawyer wants his supplementary enquiries answered, he will be dragged around from department to department only to find that the planners, surveyors, environmental health officers and housing officers are all out doing clever things with theodolites, road drills or even willow wands. Personal searches are not recommended.

One local authority, concerned to improve its rate of return of certificates of search, so geared up its operations that it was achieving a forty-eight hour turn-round on all requisitions for search. The Registrar was virtually sent to Coventry by his fellow registrars throughout the country because this level of efficiency simply could not be tolerated.

The point about all this is that, although everyone respects the majesty of the law, no one should be surprised that it tends to dawdle or, at best, proceed at a pace appropriate to its dignity. After all, the Queen is rarely seen running anywhere; Her Majesty walks slowly and occasionally pauses to speak to or shake hands with someone, and then stops to wave at the rest of us. Lawyers acting in house transactions are a bit like that. But, as we have seen, delay is not always their fault. There are local authorities to contend with, missing documents to find, those confounded gremlins to keep at bay – and then there is the Land Registry.

The registration of interests in land and the charges on it, such as leases, mortgages and other impediments, is the responsibility of HM Land Registry. Registration is compulsory nearly everywhere and, when a transaction has been completed, HM Land Registry is notified. Although the registration system has been around for a long time, there is still quite a bit of catching up to do. Registration is therefore not yet complete and, so far as one can judge, Government has not yet agreed to commit the massive resources needed to computerise the whole system.

One day, when we achieve a housing Shangri-La, buyer and seller will be able to walk into the local branch of the Land Registry, fill in a form, slap 50p on the desk and transfer will be effected by an efficient clerk with a computer. In one or two Scandinavian countries, people can virtually do that already; but not here. The system is low-tech in the strictest sense and it is not difficult to imagine how busy the Land Registry can become in boom times. Thousands of registrations a day; thousands of searches a day. It is not surprising that, every so often, someone's title is lost – as mine was when I bought, would you believe, a row of self-contained pigsties to extend my garden and protect my senses from any risk of a re-introduction of the former occupants. The same gremlins frequent the Land Registry as frequent lawyers' offices for whichever side they may be acting in a transaction.

Some of the questions the lawyers ask each other, the Register of Local Land Charges and HM Land Registry are very serious and refer to sections of Acts we never knew existed. Has the Council resolved to define the area in which the property is situated as an improvement area under S.4 of the Inner Urban Areas Act 1978? Who ever heard of that Act? The Gas Act of 1972 rears its head, as do the Control of Pollution Act 1974, the Local Government, Planning and Land Acts 1980 and hosts of Town & Country Planning Acts. Even the City of London Sewers Act of

1848, as amended by the City of London Sewers Act 1851 and the City of London (Union of Parishes) Act 1907, is still hanging about.

Fortunately, the answer to most of the questions is 'no' which means that the lawyer can direct all his attention to the occasional 'yes'. This is what lawyers are for. A good lawyer will explain to his buyer client in words of one syllable and in short crisp sentences, properly punctuated, exactly what kind of pig in a poke he is letting himself in for. Most transactions jump the legal hurdles without any difficulty but, every so often, the lawyer will find good reason to raise a warning finger.

Although this is a free country in the relative sense, we in the UK seem to have more laws which, in one way or another, restrict us than any other nation. This surfeit of restriction comes about because of our governmental sophistication. The law makers will explain that the laws do not restrict, they protect. Most statutes have built into them all kinds of appeal provisions and there are statutory devices to circumvent other statutory devices, so long as the proper procedures are followed.

The buyer's lawyer will tell him about all these things – how ancient, restrictive covenants can be overcome and how a public footpath through the front room can be legally diverted. So long as he can understand him, the buyer will realise that his lawyer is worth his weight in gold, a view which the lawyer shares. But he mustn't expect him to rush his fences; he may have to consult a whole library of reference books and ponder over some tricky legal point. If the legal point is really tricky, he may even want to consult Counsel, which will add mightily to the bill – but all of this only if you are unlucky. Most transactions, from the legal point of view, are straightforward, so long as the local authorities don't take too long with their searches and HM Land Registry doesn't lose the papers.

When contracts are exchanged, buyer and seller are bound

to complete the transaction within a period specified in the contract. That period is normally 28 days. If one of the parties backs out after contract, all kinds of dire penalties emerge and the buyer, if indeed it is he, will forfeit his 10 per cent deposit. In most cases, there is no need to worry: the process is procedural, without hitch and everyone is wreathed in smiles. The pace of it can be something of an irritation and the anxious buyer, keen to get on with his do-it-yourself redecoration programme or landscape the garden, will never find it fast enough. That is not to say that the process cannot be fast. If the circumstances justify it, lawyers have been known to proceed straight to completion – but they will still need all those answers to those questions about this and that Act.

Of course, as most properties are mortgaged, the money lenders' lawyer will add another ring to the circus. He too will need to be satisfied that the buyer is not saddling himself with some unsaleable pile. During 1990 and 1991, as recession bit deeply, unemployment rose and bankruptcies grew like poppies in a cornfield, the building societies and banks foreclosed on a large number of borrowers who could not keep up their repayments. The problem is worsening and the lenders are very much alive to the risk that they may, if the worst happens, be compelled to arrange a forced sale. No one likes a forced sale but, even at the time the buyer is buying, the risk must be borne in mind by the lender. So his lawyers will want to be sure too. The vendor's lawyer, although he will obviously seek to be helpful to his professional colleagues, is only anxious to get rid of the place on behalf of his client as quickly as possible so that his client can complete the purchase of the house to which he is moving. He then becomes the buyer's solicitor, when he will want to be absolutely sure!

Everyone involved in the house transfer game keeps saying that the purchase of a house is likely to be the biggest and most important financial transaction of a person's life. That is probably true. After all, very few of us spend £50,000, £100,000 or £150,000 in one awful lump with any kind of regularity, unless we happen to be an oil-rich sheikh who is hardly likely to be reading this anyway. The fact that house purchase is our biggest and most important financial trans-action makes it vital that we are properly advised. Advice goes beyond mere conveyancing. A good family lawyer can counsel a buyer, or indeed a seller, on a range of subjects which touch the fringes of house purchase. Lawyers too – just like estate agents – often have direct contacts with the money lenders. They know about insurance in considerable depth, particu-larly the protective insurances. This may read like tautology, but there are some insurances, such as mortgage guarantee, which can help ride future economic storms.

The point is the caring. The biggest and most important financial transaction of one's life house purchase may be – but it is also the most traumatic, the one most likely to stretch the emotions until they twang like harp strings. Except for divorce, that is; and you need a lawyer for that too. The buyer's lawyer should be seen and heard to care, and not regard his conveyancing function as a factory producing rather expensive paper. The buyer really has no one else. The estate agent, even our friendly local estate agent who has accompanied us so far, acts for the vendor. The vendor pays the estate agent's bill. To justify it, the agent will, as has been said, fawn over the buyer from the moment he is a serious applicant. He will give the impression that he is on nobody's side but the buyer's but, when the chips are down, it really has to be the vendor's side that he is on.

Solicitors would do well to remember this fact, that buyers need a shoulder to cry on or clutch at. They too should apply their wisdom to the real facts about a buyer's financial position, the security of the jobs the family holds and the real weight of hire purchase debts. Many of the present spate of foreclosures might have been unnecessary if not only legal advice, but also the wisdom of years, had been brought to bear. Too often, the factory system takes over in times of pressure and conveyancing work is delegated to clerks, who may be efficient with answers about this or that Act, but who lack the worldly experience which good lawyers are apparently born with. Solicitors should also recognise that their erudition can, if they are not careful, go right over the heads of their clients. So accustomed are they to provisos, caveats and conditions that their sentences stretch like weak elastic and contain words which many clients do not even recognise, let alone understand. Solicitors, so far as many clients are concerned, might as well be talking in Ibo or Urdu – although, in this cosmopolitan society of ours, they could as well be doing just that.

Although it is tempting to ascribe god-like qualities to them, lawyers are only human. Like our estate agent, they have things to worry about which have nothing to do with the law, even if it is only the greenfly on the roses. That is not to say that they do not have grave legal matters on their minds over and above a straightforward house transfer. They can become pre-occupied with some stretching legal problem far removed from the conveyance of number 13 Acacia Avenue and the potential fee arising from it, which is even farther removed from what our anxious buyer will pay him. But good lawyers concentrate on the job-in-hand. The only problem is that, like our estate agent, our solicitor will have dozens of other jobs going on at the same time, all at different stages, and those gremlins will be busy in the night switching papers from one file to another. Most lawyers have a quiet public dignity – except those you see rushing from court to court, holding on to their wigs, for their appearance before some crusty old judge who bawled them out the last time they were late. They have a knack of inspiring confidence – no matter what may be going on behind the scenes, no matter how delayed those damned searches in the Registers might be, no matter if that demented clerk has scattered documents all over the storage room floor.

The truth of the matter is that everyone in the house transfer game has a bad time. We know that our estate agent does: his life is piled high with trauma. No one loves the structural surveyor. The buyers and sellers reach panic condition early in the proceedings and remain in it long after completion. The money lenders at the bank worry about bridging loans in a difficult market and the money lenders of the building society worry because they are lending more to borrowers than is coming in from investors. We know about the clerks in local or national land registries who are constipated with paper. We rely on the lawyer to keep a stiff upper lip.

<table>
<tr><td>9</td><td>COMPLAINTS
DEPARTMENT</td></tr>
</table>

One of the reasons for the hysteria surrounding the whole house transfer system is the British capacity for complaint. There is even a reference book, *How to Complain*, which has become a kind of best-selling bible for the professional complainant. We British complain to each other, to local councils, to MPs – in fact, to anybody at all who will listen. We complain not only to newspapers, but also about them. Complaint about the weather is traditional, even if you aren't a farmer, but these days the range of subjects about which we complain is legion. Sadly, this condition, now reaching epidemic proportions, has become recognised by successive governments which have created new and bureaucratic systems to ensure that all complaints, however bizarre they might be, are taken absolutely seriously. There are ombudsmen for this and that and whole armies of support staff to sift the wheat from the chaff; the deadly serious from the frankly mischievous; and the awe-inspiring from the trivial. And we are now faced with the prospect of a Citizen's Charter which will introduce rights of complaint which even the most militant of us hadn't the wit to dream up.

The ombudsman (often given the dignity of a capital 'o') has become a vital part of our national way of life. The fact that we gave him a title derived from the Norse languages was, perhaps, a half-hearted attempt to underline that the whole idea was not quite British. 'Referee' might have been an alternative, but it is a title which would, admittedly, have given the poor chap a bad start because we all know what the British think about referees.

So here we are packed to the gunwales with complaints and, nowadays, with dignitaries in abundance on whom we can unload them. Complaining is official, a recognised national hobby which inspires new chapters of law and subordinate legislation when statistics prove that 'something has to be done'. That 'something has to be done' has a direct relationship to the number of complaints received about a particular subject.

Not all ombudsman organisations are officially appointed. Some are created by the professions or trades themselves to protect the public interest (you will remember that we talked about that earlier) or, at least, to give the public the right to complain. In addition to being a nation of complainers, the British are a nation of eccentrics. All ombudsmen, whether officially or privately appointed, whether one lone figure or a mass of committees or arbitrators, have learned at some cost the time-consuming activities of the determined and practised British eccentric.

There was once a lady who believed – no, knew without a shadow of a doubt – that, deep in the archives of a provincial local authority, lay documentary evidence of her right to the English throne. As if that wasn't enough, she changed her

name for each visit and had an extraordinary ability to change her appearance. Sometimes her hair was up; sometimes it was down; sometimes long; sometimes short. On some occasions, she would wear spectacles; on others, she would not. She changed her dress or her coat for each visit. The average junior clerk whose job it is to act as first filter at the reception desk is not equipped against this kind of thing and she slipped through to the higher echelons on the strength of a perfectly rational reason for the visit. Halfway through the subsequent interview about foreign bodies in marmalade or a plague of cockroaches in a local take-away – the sort of stuff local authorities thrive on – her manner would change and out would pour her imperious demands for her rights and those bits of paper allegedly down there in the vaults. She was remarkably well read. Names like Walsingham, Pitt and Disraeli would be thrown around the conversation. They had had the proof, too, and she had spoken to them all personally about it. The official's eyes would glaze over as he realised that, once again, she had caught him out.

Ombudsmen must be a bit like that – with glazed expressions in their eyes as the complaints pour in. A high proportion of the complaints they receive have no justification whatsoever, but they have probably given the complainants a bit of fun. For example, the Building Society ombudsman reported that, in the year to March 1991, he had received 2,577 complaints, a threefold increase since he was first appointed in 1987. He was good enough to say that the increase was, he thought, due to a growing public awareness of the complaints system rather than a decline in building society standards. He also said that he found for fewer than 40 per cent of the complainants. The other 60-odd per cent received bug letter number 4 in the Standard Replies Division, but after investigation, of course. One complainant, an investor, was paid £5.28p for interest lost because a building society had posted a cheque to him by second-class post. This introduces a whole new range of possibilities to the experienced and determined complainant. However, such is the level of complaint, a second building society ombudsman is to be appointed with the same powers as the first.

Of all the people in the house transfer business, the building societies are the big friendly, cuddly teddy bears. All they are there for is to give buyers bags of money with which to buy houses. Other people's money it may be, but even those other people receive quite reasonable interest on their savings. And yet there were 2,577 complaints about them, over eight a day if you discount Sundays.

The number of complaints against building socities is modest compared with the number received against solicitors by the Solicitors' Complaints Bureau. There are, of course, more solicitors than there are building societies and that probably accounts for the fact that, in 1990, there were about 18,000 complaints to the Bureau. Assuming that solicitors don't work on Saturdays, Sundays or Bank Holidays, that is approaching 70 complaints each working day. Not all of the complaints were made by the general public. In fact, 4,000 complaints were made by solicitors about other solicitors. These would make interesting reading.

The man with most complaints on his mind is Sir Gordon Borrie QC, at present the Director-General of Fair Trading. In 1991, he agreed, one suspects without a great deal of enthusiasm, to continue in office for another year. In his annual report for 1990, he wrote that the 700,000 consumer complaints which he received during the year were, in his view, 'the tip of the iceberg'. Now most of us thought we knew about icebergs: about two thirds under water and the top bit glistening in the Arctic sun. Sir Gordon's iceberg is different. His iceberg has only one per cent above water – which means that 69,300,000 complaints just hang about going nowhere, all bottled up inside furious breasts which are merely beaten from time to time out of pure anger and frustration. There is no reason for that. Sir Gordon wants all those 69,300,000 complainants to get their complaints off their chests by writing to him. There are a few property developers who probably have great sympathy with Sir Gordon's view. If the Office of Fair Trading received 70 million complaints every year, the staff needed would mop up all that surplus empty office space in London, Royal Mail profits would be dramatically increased and a few more forests would tumble somewhere in the world.

Conjecture is a wasteful pastime, so let us stick to this figure of 700,000 complaints. Sir Gordon is no square. He lists his own Top Twenty, but with not a hint of Madonna. Right at the top of the list is the used car fraternity, who scored a hefty 64,727. Now there's a surprise! TVs and electrical goods muster 54,078, closely followed by food and drink with 53,357. Double glazing comes a sorry 11th with only 21,534 complaints – and, right at the bottom of Sir Gordon's list, just scraping in at number 20, is entertainment/catering/accommodation with a puny 9,989. Estate agents aren't even in Sir Gordon's Top Twenty, despite all the odium, all the complicated legislation and all the brouhaha that goes on about them. Only a modest 1,571 complaints were recorded in the year of report, a reduction of 2.2 per cent on the previous year. This figure is at about the same level as complaints about lawyers received in Sir Gordon's office, 1,452, although you will remember that the lawyers' own ombudsman received 18,000 complaints, including 4,000 from other lawyers, and is so overworked that he is to be supplemented by another. Roughly at the same level come water and domestic fuel, solid and liquid; prams are up there in the 7,000s along with packaged holidays.

The report tries to explain the form of the complaints about estate agents but, to be fair, tabular presentation covering sixty categories of goods or services doesn't lend itself to easy explanation. Of the 1,571 complaints about agents, 294 were about substandard service, 84 were about non-completion of service, 856 were about selling techniques; misleading claims, representations or advertisements, or lack of information; and three were on the subject of health or safety. The fact is that the highest number of complaints – 856 and this is well over half – made about estate agents come into the category of 'selling techniques; misleading claims, representations or advertisements; or lack of information.' These smack of buyers' complaints, those who don't actually pay for the services they receive. Is there, the agents are entitled to ask, no justice?

The new regulations, which we will come to in a minute, are insistent upon the vendor being told precisely what costs lie in wait for him. Although it is difficult to analyse precisely how many complaints relate to the fees which agents charge, it is reasonable to assume that a proportion of the complaints are written following receipt of that awful bill. Even if fees are not high on the list of complaints mentioned by Sir Gordon, the subject is certainly aired with some venom in pubs, clubs and anywhere else people might congregate. It might be sensible to examine the 'money for old rope' attitude and measure UK agency fees against those charged in other countries. We have already noted that UK fees are variable and, because there is severe competition for instructions, even what we regarded once as standard scales are being trimmed just to attract business. A fee of one and a half per cent of the sale price is now common but, as we all know, some agents who are anxious for work are sometimes prepared to halve that fee level. In America, estate agents charge up to six per cent of the agreed sale price. In France, the fee can be as high as fourteen per cent – but the coffee is probably better. It is difficult to find a European country in which estate agents' fees are lower than those in the Southern half of England. There is some talk that fees are lower in the Low Countries but there are few of us who would prefer to live there anyway.

Not content with the disciplinary procedures of the professional bodies covering estate agency practice, a group of the larger institutional chains of estate agents has got together and appointed its own ombudsman. A cynic might suggest that this is a device to give complainants their head without letting them anywhere near Sir Gordon Borrie and his Office of Fair Trading. Sir Gordon has a beady eye for what are known as 'triggers' – offences which draw attention to an agency practice and 'trigger off' a full-scale investigation which could result in a total ban or even prison. We will soon examine the full pageantry of the law as it affects estate agency and 'triggers' will figure hugely in our summary.

The professional bodies still have their codes of conduct and a system of disciplinary committees who investigate complaints. Their ultimate sanction is dismissal from the club. Since the emergence of degrees and diplomas which give partial or total exemption from the professional examinations of the societies, dismissal from the club is not regarded as all that serious. It is unlikely to have dramatic effect on someone's capacity to earn a living. In any event, an already confused public is unlikely to ask a graduate boasting a degree in estate management if he were once a member of the RICS, ISVA or the NAEA and has been clobbered by the disciplinary committee. But Sir Gordon is different. He can really hurt.

10 THE FUNDING SOURCES

Building societies are the primary source of funding for house purchase in this country. We have all been persuaded by the television advertising that the building societies are staffed by girls who have an extraordinary resemblance to Bo Derek and who are only there to please, particularly if you are an investor and can dance like Fred Astaire. Recently, advertisements have included a health warning, a bit like those on cigarette packets. 'Failure' they say, 'to maintain repayments may result in your losing your home'. Well, we know all that, but let us, first of all, look on the bright side.

The house purchase arrangements enjoyed by the great British public so far as money is concerned are the subject of envy. In many countries, lenders spread the risk. A potential buyer may have to go to two, even three, sources for his money. Not so here – but this discounts Grandma, Dad or whoever else it is the buyer taps for the deposit money or even the whole difference between the agreed price and the loan offer. So let us be thankful that we have building societies.

The system is delightfully simple. Those people who are already housed, and have somehow contrived to spend less than they earn, actually save money. Some are reckless; some gamble on the Stock Exchange, become names at Lloyd's or back losers in horse and dog races; there is not much difference. Some put their money into higher rate deposit accounts at the bank and others put their money into the building societies. Doting grandparents sometimes open building society accounts for their offspring's offspring at the time of the christening, thus encouraging a strong urge to save as the children do their paper rounds, odd jobs or extract more pocket money from Dad.

There is plenty of competition for savers' money. Even the Government offers zealous savers all kinds of tax-free incentives if they invest in saving certificates or premium bonds. The building societies have, however, a good steady image – and, if you think about it, there is something socially acceptable about lending your money so that others can borrow to buy a home. So the savers save by putting their surplus cash into a building society at an agreed level of interest. The building society then lends it to borrowers for house purchase at a higher rate of interest; to secure the loan, the building society takes a charge on the property as mortgagee, and the borrower becomes the mortgagor. In fact, the mortgagee grabs the deeds and puts them in the vaults, where we all hope and pray they can be found when the debt is repaid. We have had enough of the disaffected and demented clerks who strew documents all over the floor.

There are, of course, some snags. We have already discussed the building society survey and valuation. It may be that a sale price of £60,000 has been agreed, subject, of course, to contract and structural survey. The building society survey and valuation may disclose that, in the opinion of the surveyor/valuer, the house, bungalow or flat would be worth only £55,000 if the mortgagee were to force a sale in the open market, in the event of the borrower defaulting on his repayments. That may not be so bad so long as the borrower can rustle up the difference – not forgetting that he also has to rustle up legal fees, stamp duty, removal expenses, perhaps some furniture, and you can bet a pound to a penny that none of the curtains or carpets from the old house will fit. But there is another problem: those dreadful words 'subject to status'.

Building societies don't just lend willy-nilly. They will want to know all about the 'status' of the borrower. This has nothing to do with knighthoods or membership of the Rotary

Club. This is a hard-nosed appraisal of the applicant's finances supported by employer's and banker's references. The societies' officials know all about economics and formulae have been developed which indicate what the applicant can afford in the way of monthly repayments. The operative word is 'multiple': the applicant's annual earnings (husband and wife sometimes jointly, sometimes not) are calculated and the society offers a multiple of those earnings as the maximum advance. Practice varies between societies and varies, too, according to how flush the societies are at a particular time. At worst, a society may say that they will offer three times the earnings of the husband and one times the earnings of the wife. If the husband is earning £14,000 a year and the wife is earning £12,000 a year, the couple will be offered £54,000 which, you will remember, is £1,000 short of the required amount. Where prices are dramatically higher than our basic £60,000, such as in some parts of London, the 'status' factor becomes serious. If a borrower and his wife, even though the society is prepared to offer three times the earnings of both, want to borrow, say, £240,000, they have to be earning £80,000 a year between them. Not an easy target – unless you are a chairman of a newly privatised industry.

We must, however, stick to the realism of the £60,000 house. The valuation of a house is a tricky business. The estate agent will have fixed the sale price with the vendor – probably after some haggling because the vendor wants as much as he can get, whereas the agent is unlikely to want a house on his books which is extravagantly over-priced. He just won't be able to sell it. Over-pricing is not so silly in a rising market, but it can be disastrous when the market is falling fast. Only occasionally a house, perhaps because of its outstanding beauty, will defy a falling market and remain attractive to a particular class of buyer; but don't rely on it. The agent will know which way the market is going and he will fix a price which reflects it, warning the vendor that he should be prepared to accept a lower figure. The attitude at this stage of the game is 'let's give it a try and see what happens'.

The building society's valuer is not of the same persuasion. His responsibility is to the building society and his valuation will take into account the direction of the market, too. And don't forget the forced sale factor: his valuation is likely to be harsh in comparison with the agent's 'let's give it a try' approach and nowhere near the vendor's hopes. All of this is very irritating because the buyer is paying for the building society survey and valuation anyway. It is also important to remember that the survey is not a true structural survey, although that doesn't seem to matter to the building society.

Building societies offer loans on normal monthly repayment terms. Repayments cover capital and interest and the capital borrowed is slowly eroded over the borrowing term. Societies now offer a range of mortgage types, always subject to status; for example, a low-start mortgage where the early repayments are low, as one would expect, will suit the rising star whose promise is high earnings in a few years' time. This is a fairly demanding judgement in the early 1990s, when rising stars in the City of London shoot downwards at an alarming rate. Often, there is complaint that societies are slow to drop interest rates to borrowers after the base rate falls. We have to remember that societies are always facing serious competition for investors' funds. If they drop the level of interest they pay to their own lenders, those fickle investors can swing their funds to a more attractive medium and there would be no money to lend to worried house buyers.

Unsecured repayment mortgages are a worry for borrowers. If the breadwinner dies in the middle of the mortgage term, there is a risk that the house will have to be sold, unless life assurance cover has been arranged. Mortgages linked to endowment assurance are therefore recommended. These assure the life or lives of the breadwinner or breadwinners so that the borrower(s) pay only the interest on the loan for the term of the borrowing. The endowment insurance premiums are paid and (so long as they are up-to-date) at the end of the term, the assurance company pays off the debt. Endowment policies can be 'with' or 'without' profits, the latter being the least expensive. A 'with profits' policy can produce something of a bonanza at the end of the borrowing term and a check on comparative performance is prudent before committing oneself to a particular assurance company.

Most building societies expect the borrower to insure the mortgaged property through them. There are two reasons for this. First, they want to be sure that the premiums are paid; after all, they are unlikely to be very pleased if they inherit a pile of charred bricks in the event that the place burns down and the owner has forgotten to pay the insurance premium. Secondly, they receive a commission from the insurance company on the premium value – a nice little earner, if ever there was one.

There is also something called 'bridging', which every buyer who is also a seller has to know about. As we have seen, and our friendly local estate agent is painfully aware of this, particularly when it comes to cash flow, nothing in house transfer happens at just the right time. A buyer who is also a seller is bent on selling his present house at just the right moment to enable him to buy. In a buoyant market, there is a good chance that he will achieve his aim – with a little luck and a bit of shouting at the lawyers; in a dormant, depressed or near dead market, the odds lengthen dramatically. The chances of his selling his old house before he has to complete the purchase of his new one are slim. It seems to happen like that, no matter how clever you are; the time gap can be months or, dare one say it, years.

In those circumstances, a determined buyer will be paying his mortgage repayments on the new house as well as on the old one, and he will not have received any capital from his sale because he hasn't sold anything except his soul to the money lenders. He will, therefore – and this doesn't apply to the really rich – need a bridging loan. This is a loan to bridge the gap between the purchase of the new and the disposal of the old. The time gap is piled high with debts and it is no good offering lawyers or structural engineers IOUs. Banks are the normal source of bridging loans. The friendly, listening bank manager will do all he can to help anyone in this predicament – so long as he is satisfied that the loan is secured down to the borrower's last drop of blood. It is wise to settle any bridging arrangements before completing the purchase of another house and that might mean that the vendor, who is buying a house somewhere else, will have to go to his bank for a bridging loan. The principle is simply: better him than me. Bridging can be expensive. It can add another stratum of stress on the layers which developed from the moment of the first tentative step into an estate agent's office – and there were already a few layers of stress from just talking about it, selecting a location and trying to do the sums when the pocket calculator is playing up.

All this debt calls for the services of another professional who charges fees, the tax accountant. It is vital to ensure that every scrap of tax relief is garnered – at a time when there is a growing belief that, such is their avidity, tax inspectors are actually working on commission and achieve bonuses for exceptional extortion.

His Royal Highness, Prince Philip, Duke of Edinburgh, has chaired a serious study into homelessness which has recommended the phased abandonment of tax relief for house purchase. The theory is that such a policy would suck in so much money to the Exchequer that the standard rate of income tax would fall like a stone and there would still be enough in the kitty to house all the homeless. So far as I can judge, no one has yet canvassed all those millions of mortgagors living on tight budgets who calculated their outgoings to the last pound. They are unlikely to be convinced that they will benefit from the theory and, as they are voters as well as mortgagors, they might just rebel. It could be disastrous for a party seeking to win an election: 'Well, dear friends', the candidate might say, 'although we are removing tax relief on house purchase loans, we do have British Rail wanting umpteen millions – sorry, billions – and the health service could do with a few quid, so we can't reduce income tax.' That would go down like a lead balloon.

The community charge, if you remember, had much the same effect. The government of the day introduced it without explaining in detail the evils and unfairness of the then rating system. A large slice of the population, particularly the well-to-do, found themselves much better off under the community charge arrangements and said absolutely nothing, not even 'thank you'. But there were riots, protests, refusals to pay and all kinds of mayhem from those who were not better off, although we know that many of the protesters had never paid a penny towards the public services and, by the look of them, would be unlikely to do so in the future.

It would be surprising if any political party actually seeking power has the nerve to withdraw such tax relief, particularly with the polls showing the two main parties so close and the third party poised to hold the balance of power. So don't worry about it for the time being; there is quite enough to worry about as it is. The Secretary of State for the Environment has, as promised, tampered with what we and Wat Tyler called the poll tax and is to introduce the Council Tax, a system of rating based on bands of value which are fairly tightly drawn. House-proud owners who know they will want to sell their house in two or three years' time may prefer to sit in a higher band so that their apparent values are higher. Buyers will look at the Council Tax bands and, if the property is priced well above the band it is in, will turn to a house which isn't. The system will add another burden to the shoulders of our friendly local estate agent but, as he may have been asked by the government to help in setting the values, he might well be in the Bahamas anyway.

The main point to make is that it is vital to sort out the housing finance as soon as possible. It is no earthly good saying it is only money. It is rather more than that: it is stress, tension, argument – a whole package of things which bring on world-weariness even in 22-year olds. It is a good idea in any business to plan for crisis management. This is a method of fearing the worst and knowing exactly what to do when it happens. It seems a long time ago that we said that, seeing we change houses on an average once every six or seven years, we come as lambs to the slaughter, simply because we have forgotten what it was like the time before. It is probably worth the fee to have a chat with your lawyer, asking him for a comprehensive list of the disasters which might befall the transaction. We have been through all the problems that might arise up to the point of exchange of contracts. Most buyers and sellers breathe a sigh of relief at this stage. Hold your breath. Your buyer, even though he has signed the contract and paid his deposit, can still decide not to complete.

To be fair, this does not happen all that often. But it could happen to you if you have that kind of luck; that is what crisis management is about. Although you have the 10 per cent deposit, your sums are still 90 per cent short of what you thought you were going to have at the time you bought your new house. It is therefore sensible to make contingency bridging arrangements with your bank. Failure to complete is not the only risk which justifies such arrangements; in a poor market, failure to sell at all before you move to your new home is probably the greatest risk of all. You could, of course, issue a writ for specific performance on the contract if your buyer fails to complete. It is never wise to bank on the outcome of any civil action and, in any event, such actions can take a long time. You might be moving into your retirement lease home by the time your action is finished.

None of this is intended to knock the basic funding system. The building societies – British to the core – look kindly on first-time buyers especially if they have been saving with them like mad things from the cradle. Both banks and building societies have a burning desire to lend money for house purchase and the resulting competition has created a range of lending packages for the first-time buyer. Discounts on interest rates for an agreed period are offered by many societies and banks. Fixed rates of interest for agreed terms are another carrot. The message, of course, is to shop around to get the best deal possible just as, when you are saving, it is wise to find out who is offering the best rates of interest. This book is not a brochure and it would be folly to point to a particular scheme offered by this or that building society or bank, simply because it might be overtaken by another tomorrow. So do your own shopping. So long as they are not tied to a particular lending institution, your professional help will advise you.

Don't go away, but this could be the longest chapter. Recent changes in the law relating to estate agency practice herald what has been described as 'a new régime'. The components of that régime affect estate agents, their staffs, a few other people – even dear Myrtle who still can't stick those photographs on straight – and those they serve in one way or another, the sellers and buyers. We know already that our friendly, local estate agent has had a fairly rugged time of it trying to earn an honest crust, but the legal requirements which now surround him make it worse.

It can, and no doubt will, be argued that, such is the complexity of modern society, the consumer has to be protected. It is well known that the consumer is not very skilled at protecting himself and equally well known that there are those around who will exploit ignorance to their personal benefit. Most estate agents are honest, straightforward and upright in their dealings with buyers and sellers alike and are sufficiently aware of the law to follow good business practice. Some are not like that and it is that handful of sharp operators which has brought agency generally into disrepute. They are the primary target of the estate agency legislation which this chapter seeks to summarise, but obviously it affects all estate agents, good, bad and indifferent. For the good, the legislation will further complicate lives which are already complicated enough, as we have seen; for the bad, it will probably send them out of the business altogether, which no one will mourn. The indifferent won't have read anything about the legal requirements and will be surprised when they receive a warning (if they bother to read it at all) from our old friend, the Director-General of Fair Trading.

We have explained how the Estate Agents Act of 1979 came into being. The Act gave power for the introduction of regulations and orders to spell out the detail of what the parliamentary draftsman forgot to put in the original Act. You will find that there is a power to make orders and regulations in most Acts of Parliament. It is a wonderful catch-all in case the draftsman has forgotten something – although these draftsmen are people of formidable intellect. Occasionally, they suffer emotional stress and don't concentrate as much as they should, probably because they are in the middle of a house sale and purchase transaction.

The Director-General of Fair Trading has responsibility under the Estate Agents Act 1979 for administering certain regulatory provisions, whereby estate agents may be banned or warned for various offences or malpractices. He also has a statutory duty under the Act to keep under review and to advise the Secretary of State on the working and enforcement of the Act, and on social and commercial developments in the United Kingdom relating to the carrying on of estate agency work and related activities. As long ago as 1988, the Office of Fair Trading issued a review of the 1979 Act indicating where greater consumer protection was required. There was a little to-ing and fro-ing and in September 1989 the Director-General issued a consultation document. This was sent to all of the professional bodies representing estate agency, to consumer and trading standards bodies and to a host of other interested people. The consultation document sought increased consumer protection. Although there was some modest tempering of what the Director-General proposed, the result has been the issue of regulations which require the estate agent to do certain things, not to do certain things and, generally, to behave himself in a seemly manner.

Before we go on to all of those regulations, it is perhaps

worth discussing one thing which the Director-General did not do: he did not recommend minimum standards of competence before an estate agent could practise. We have been through all that and we know that the RICS and ISVA have tough examination systems. We know that there are diplomas and degrees in estates subjects which, broadly, qualify someone to advise others through subject knowledge. The major professional bodies are not anxious to see large numbers of people deciding to be estate agents, not only because of the question of competition, but also because they seriously believe that you have to know more about the house transfer system, the economics of house ownership and the construction of houses than can be gleaned from looking at the advertisements in the local newspaper. The Director-General would have none of this; although there was considerable pressure from within the industry and from certain consumer bodies for the introduction of minimum standards of competence for estate agents, he remained sceptical. It was contended by some that most of the malpractices in the industry stem from new entrants lacking appropriate qualifications or experience. The Director-General's office had little or no evidence to support this view. Indeed, some of the complaints received were about agents who had been in the business for many years; nor were they confined to agents who had no professional qualifications.

There is just a hint that, at some time in the future, a licensing system might be introduced. For the moment, it is recognised that such a scheme would be costly to introduce and administer and would also require primary legislation for which there is little time in either House. So the Office of Fair Trading is not, so far, persuaded that a licensing system is justified. All that we have after all this weighty consultation are the Estate Agents (Undesirable Practices) Order, the Estate Agents (Provision of Information) Regulations and a few others. That package of orders and regulations was, at one time, to include the misdescription of property by estate agents. This aspect is now covered by the Property Misdescriptions Act 1991.

We have been through the awful process which vendor, buyer, agent and all the rest must follow. To make the law easier to understand, it seems sensible to relate the law to that awful process. So we will start with the estate agent's visit to his vendor. In addition to measuring and describing the building, falling on that damned roller-skate and pointing out that front gardens resembling jungles are a positive hindrance to a quick sale, our estate agent now has to obey the law. You will remember that our estate agent could, according to the vendor's whim, be appointed as sole agent, joint sole agent or multiple agent. We warned about certain phrases which the agent might slip into the conversation. Everything – for everyone's sake – must now be written down.

Under The Estate Agents (Provision of Information) Regulations, 1991, if the agent uses the words 'sole selling rights', he must inform the vendor in writing in the following way:

Sole Selling Rights

You will be liable to pay remuneration to us, in addition to any other costs or charges agreed, in each of the following circumstances:

If conditional contracts for the sale of the property are exchanged in the period during which we have sole selling rights, even if the purchaser was not found by us but by another agent or by any other person, including yourself;

If unconditional contracts for the sale of the property are exchanged after the expiry of the period during which we have sole selling rights but to a purchaser who was introduced to you during that period or with whom we had negotiations about the property during that period.

If he uses the words 'sole agency', the agent must inform the vendor in writing, so:

Sole Agency

You will be liable to pay remuneration to us, in addition to any other costs or charges agreed, if at any time unconditional contracts for the sale of the property are exchanged:

With a purchaser introduced by us during the period of our sole agency or with whom we had negotiations about the property during that period;

Or

With a purchaser introduced by another agent during that period.

And, if the agent uses the phrase 'ready, willing and able purchaser', the written explanation must read:

Ready, Willing and Able Purchaser

A purchaser is a 'ready, willing and able' purchaser if he is prepared and is able to exchange unconditional contracts for the purchase of your property.

You will be liable to pay remuneration to us, in addition to any other costs or charges agreed, if such a purchaser is introduced by us in accordance with your instructions and this must be paid even if you subsequently withdraw and unconditional contracts for sale are not exchanged, irrespective of your reasons.

Note: There is a Scottish version of these explanations to take account of Scottish law.

Already, under the original Estate Agents Act 1979, agents are required to inform the vendors of the fees and other charges for which they will be liable, even if the standard 'no sale, no fee' arrangements apply. We have already discussed what services the vendor can expect the agent to give, but these now have to be spelled out in words of one syllable, so that they can be easily understood. In some areas, the agent will ask the vendor to pay for advertising, and this now has to be stated clearly and unequivocably. If the agent is to be appointed as a 'sole agent', any time limit should be clearly stated so that there is no misunderstanding.

When the 1979 Act was first passed, it has to be said that many estate agents took it very seriously. Their managers and negotiators, when they called on vendors to take instructions, went round with all kinds of triple carbon notice sheets which the vendor was expected to read, understand and even sign. One copy was for the vendor to keep, one copy was for the agent's own file on the transaction and the other one went into a ring binder, with all of the other signed instructions, just in case anybody sinister asked to see them. Those managers and negotiators had a rough time. You know the kind of thing:

What's this then?

Well, it's your instruction to me to sell the house for you – it sets out the fee payable, what we'll do for you and the other charges for which you are liable.

Have I got to read **all** of this?

It's only eight lines . . .

Eight lines – I can't read all that. I've got to get on with me pools – it's Wednesday.

It's really very simple . . .

It don't look simple to me. What's this word here mean?

Don't forget that, on his first visit to take instructions, the agent has quite a lot to do. He has, as a primary task, to give the vendor confidence; discussions about long documents, which the agent may insist the vendor must sign to show he understands and accepts the terms, are not conducive to giving confidence. If the agent slips in that it is a requirement of the law, it is often like a red rag to a bull: 'The law! I won't sign anything to do with the law – you never know what they'll have you for.'

In those early days of the 1979 Act, managers and negotiators who returned from every instruction visit with a signed chit were looked upon with some awe by their contemporaries. Since the latest regulations came into force, a success rate of 100 per cent would justify a medal from the National Association of Estate Agents. Whereas eight lines were once sufficient, the requirement is now for at least an A4 page of print. Few vendors are proficient in rapid reading and the taking of instructions could now be a seriously extended occupation. In the good old days, our friendly local estate agent would rush off to his instruction appointment equipped simply with a notebook and pencil, a tape measure and a camera (having checked on the film). He now has to go armed with a battery of forms and the knowledge that he must, if he is wise, persuade a recalcitrant vendor to sign something which, if he actually has the time to read it, he is unlikely to understand and even less likely to want to sign even if he had to; and that's not the end of it.

We have recorded in these pages how the large financial houses – the building societies and insurance companies – entered the world of estate agency. We have also seen how estate agents add to the list of instructions to sell and the lists of budding buyers. The new regulations (and, remember, this is consumer protection legislation) require that the client must be informed of any services provided which result in the payment of fees to the estate agent or any associated company. Even personal commissions to a member of the estate agent's staff must be disclosed. Disclosure must be in writing and, as the client will, undoubtedly, lose his copy and deny ever having had it, the estate agent might even consider recorded delivery or personal hand delivery on signature. Worse, the estate agent must obtain confirmation of the instruction from the client in the light of the new circumstances. A wise estate agent will ensure that confirmation is in writing: another form, another bit of dialogue, another slab of time.

What sort of things are the regulations aimed at? When a budding applicant with a house to sell takes an interest in one of our estate agent's houses for sale, it must dawn on our estate agent, if he has any wits at all, that the potential buyer is also a potential seller; that, if the agent plays his cards right, means another sale and another fee. The agent selling a house for a vendor must pass on all offers received – and we have seen how the agent who knows all about the financial circumstances of his applicants might be asked to advise the vendor which offer to accept. If a buyer has the makings of a vendor as well, it is in the estate agent's interests to push that buyer forward – although he mustn't. If the vendor knows about this interest, he will judge the estate agent's advice accordingly.

If a buyer has agreed to borrow or take out insurance from a building society or insurance company which happens to own the estate agency selling the house, this arrangement must also be notified to the vendor. Again, this is because the profits accruing to the agency owner might just cloud the advice of the estate agent when he and the vendor decide which offer to accept.

We all know that a buyer's circumstances can change in the middle of a negotiation. Life is like that. A buyer who, at first interview, indicates that he has all his money in tenners under the mattress, might smoke in bed and remove a sizeable portion of his fortune. He therefore suddenly needs a small advance to top up the residue – and our friendly estate agent arranges it. Even if our estate agent is not owned by a building society or insurance company, he might be 'tied' to one or other and receive a commission. And this might happen when a deal has already been struck, subject to contract and structural survey, of course. The vendor still has to be told.

The chances are that the vendor won't particularly want to be told, but he will have to put up with it. After all, it's the law in all its majesty looking after his personal interests as a consumer. In fact, the vendor, faced with all these bits of paper which he is expected to read, understand and even sign, is likely to be just a little more confused than the estate agent who, two or three years ago, thought he had the whole job taped. The estate agent, whose need for filing cabinets and storage space has probably now increased threefold, is likely to become morose and petulant, because he believes that no one is ever going to look at all this paper ever again.

Well, the agent could be wrong. To understand why he might be wrong, we have to examine the 'triggers' which, if pulled (or, as we professionals used to say, squeezed), create all kinds of excitement at the Office of Fair Trading. It is not unreasonable to say that our poor friendly local estate agent is in something of a daze. Don't forget, he has all these deals, many of them in chains from Wick to Weymouth, and all are at different stages. Earlier, we described a local authority local land charges clerk as a demented ant; beside an estate agent coping with the new regulations, he will appear almost indolent.

Even the once reliable marketing aids such as 'For Sale' boards have taken something of a battering. The old grizzled estate agency hands knew that 'getting your board up' meant a lot. People on the move often made a tour of their selected area in the family saloon. If they saw a preponderance of 'For Sale' boards or 'Sold' boards displaying the name of the same firm, the chances were strong that they would pay a call on that firm first. We described earlier the sneaky habits of some agents of slipping their boards into a virtual forest of boards outside a simple villa and relying on percentage odds that their boards would catch a buyer's eye.

All of that has stopped. In October 1987, there was a governmental clamp-down on the size and number of estate agency boards outside houses and flats. The size of boards was cut to a quarter, which meant that no board could be larger than three feet by two feet six inches or half a square metre. Two agents advertising the same property would be allowed to share a slightly larger board, but the basic rule was one house, one board. The government was not too draconian: agents were allowed a whole year to make arrangements for the change. You can imagine the uproar in the agency world. The establishment figures in the professional bodies puffed a bit and said that it was correct environmentally; at the sharp end of the business, the managers and negotiators bought running shoes. Nowadays, of course, the wily agent, off on that first 'instruction' visit, slips a board into the boot of his car and hopes, if the vendor agrees to sign everything he has to sign, that he can bang a nail into the front gate on the way out. In that way, he could be first in the race to get up that single board. By the time the other multiple agents have got their act together, he could have sold the place. This may be unlikely in a dormant market, but at least he has his board up to attract the attention of potential buyers and other sellers.

Agency boards have even found their way into the House of Lords (no, the House wasn't for sale). In the case Porter v Honey, their lordships decided that an estate agent who lawfully placed a 'For Sale' board on a property did not commit a criminal offence when, subsequently, another estate agent, without the knowledge or consent of the first estate agent, placed a second 'For Sale' board on the same property. So there; all the more reason for our estate agent to slip that board, a hammer and six-inch nail into the boot of his car.

It is no good agents supposing that no one will notice that there are two or three boards outside a house; someone will. You will remember all those 700,000 complaints pouring into the Office of Fair Trading which represent, according to the Director-General, only one per cent of the total. Only a few months ago, two Hampstead agents were each fined £300 and £172.50p costs for erecting 'For Sale' boards in Camden. Admittedly, they chose to put them up in a conservation area, but the principle is the same. Somebody had noticed.

The 'trigger' system relies on the fact that somebody will notice. The original list of triggers was really quite straightforward. Most estate agents had a fair idea whether or not circumstances were likely to trigger an onslaught from the OFT. They would know, for example, if they had been convicted of any offence involving fraud or other dishonesty or violence. They would be less sure, perhaps, about offences under the Estate Agents Act, but they would know if they had obstructed a trading standards officer. They would also know if they had committed an offence under the 'client account regulations'.

We haven't mentioned this before, but estate agents must keep clients' money in a separate account which attracts interest. Every good estate agent was doing this long before there were regulations anyway. Any small business needs management accounting and the risk of confusing fees with deposits was too awful to contemplate for those who had any sense of propriety. So, as some agents didn't keep separate accounts and some had even been known to run off with amassed deposits, regulations were introduced. To offend them triggers retribution from above.

Since the passing of the Estate Agents (Specified Offences) Order 1991, there are another 34 triggers added to the list and then later there will be, no doubt, a few more under the Property Misdescriptions Act 1991. Most of these new triggers are taken from other consumer protection legislation. Sex and race are among them and any estate agent who accepts instructions from a sexist racist – and there are a few about – seriously risks his agency future. It is not difficult for both vendor and agent to get into trouble on grounds of race or sex, and even both. It happens in furnished lettings offices frequently. A landlord will say, 'I'm not letting to three men – they'll never clean the place'. That's sexist. If the three men happen to differ in colour from the landlord, it is hard to prove that it is not racist, too. The agent is in the middle of all this.

That is all by the way; for the moment, we are still trying to persuade the vendor to read, understand and sign the form. We learned earlier that the agent will begin to notice points about the house from the moment he sees it. His professional senses will be all aquiver as he sees the slipped tile on the roof, the awful garden and the fact that, in a moment of aberration, the owner has painted the front door phosphorescent ultramarine. He is now likely to be far too preoccupied with his documentation and the rehearsal of his explanations of 'interests' beyond his estate agency work. It must be sensible for him to get all of this out of the way before he even looks at the house, measures it up and makes notes for his detailed particulars of sale.

In this case, because our local friendly estate agent is so nice and the vendor is the world's most reasonable man, we will assume that the form is read, understood and even signed. It would be nice to think that, apart from selling the wretched house, this would be the end of notifications, signing and revised instructions. Not a bit of it. As we have said, if the agent, his owning company, a member of his staff – it is difficult to know where to stop – derives a commission, payment or other benefit arising from the instruction, he has to tell the vendor. The vendor can then consider whether he wants to vary his instructions.

Some agents, although our friendly agent is far too nice and professional for this kind of thing, have a hot line to removal firms, double-glazing salesmen, builders and decorators, carpet suppliers, electrical goods retailers – all manner of people. And those people, if they secure business or sales from their notifications, slip the agent an agreed commission for the favour. The strict letter of the law demands that the vendor shall be told – and the fact of the telling, with a supporting signature of the vendor if possible, has to be logged. If the principle of the law is examined, it is not difficult to understand why the vendor should be told. An agent who has sold a house to a buyer financed by a building society which owns the agency with an endowment assurance policy on which the agent receives a commission, and who is willing to use the agent's recommended removal people and buy his carpets and telly through the agent's suggested suppliers, might be regarded as being biased in any recommendation he might make to his vendor. In a poor market, the vendor is only too anxious to sell. He probably won't care about all this, although he might be tempted to try to reduce the agent's bill at the end of the day as the agent's commissions mount up. But he has to be told and the telling has to be logged, just in case one of the trigger offences brings the Office of Fair Trading down on the agent like the proverbial ton of bricks.

We haven't even reached the Property Misdescriptions Act yet. In March 1990, the Office of Fair Trading issued a report suggesting a long list of matters of description about which a false statement should give rise to an offence under the Trade Descriptions Act. That suggestion was overtaken by the Property Misdescriptions Act, but the list is likely to remain. It covers location or address; aspect and proximity to places or amenities; facilities; proximity to, and availability of, any services; tenure; nature and characteristics of title; in the case of leasehold property, the length of the lease (including any unexpired term); amount of any ground rent or chief rent; rateable value or community charge; structural characteristics; amount of any service charge; conformity or compliance with any standard, regulations, guarantee or scheme; accommodation; measurements and sizes; physical characteristics, including construction, appearance or fittings; fitness for purpose, strength or condition; survey, inspection, investigation by any person and the effects or results thereof; person by whom any building, fixture, component or thing was manufactured, designed, produced, processed or reconditioned; fixtures (whether moveable or not) included in or excluded from sale; previous history, including the age, ownership and use of any building, fixture, component or thing; treatments, processing, repairs, improvements and the effects and results thereof; restricted covenants, including restrictions on resale; easements; existence or nature of planning permission; and the existence and extent of any listed building status.

Our heart goes out to the estate agent, still sucking his pencil, who has to be sure that every word he writes cannot be challenged. Goodbye 'immaculate'; goodbye 'prestigious'. Well, perhaps that is no bad thing. 'Close to buses, shops and schools' will have to be checked against reality. Anything which smacks of subjectivity or opinion must be regarded with the utmost suspicion. The average house described honestly, with no poetic licence at all, is likely to lift no hearts; and it is no good relying on the photograph (even if there was a film in the camera) because that would be so dark and misty that it would offer no relief from bald description. Potential buyers will sit at home reading through all this turgid stuff, gradually realising that they would probably be far happier staying put. Goodness knows what all of this is going to do to the housing market. Many, in 1990 and 91, said it could not get worse; it could.

Much will, of course, depend on the Office of Fair Trading and the manner of its policing of the Act and Regulations.

There should be no need for armies of investigative henchmen checking up on procedural misdemeanours, gasping at the excessive use of adjectives, detecting some undisclosed fringe commission or discovering that it is Myrtle's Gran's little cottage that the office sold last week. After all, the complaints will still roll in and, if the OFT has its way, they will become a flood of 1.2 complaints per man, woman and child per year and rising. This will be quite enough for the OFT to get its teeth into.

Perhaps you don't want to be an estate agent after all. It wouldn't surprise me.

12 THE COMMERCIAL SIDE OF AGENCY

We have been, up to now, concerned only with the activities of the residential estate agent, the vendors to whom he is responsible and the hosts of budding buyers on whom he lavishes extraordinary care and attention. We have examined his derivation, his methods and the new laws and regulations with which he now has to comply. While the complaints were mounting up against the residential agents and the dramatic changes of ownership of agency were taking place, the commercial estate agents – those who handle offices, shops, factories and warehouses – stood aloof from the odium as though it had nothing to do with them. I'm afraid it does.

Those who know, so far as anyone *can* know where new law is concerned, have said that both residential and commercial agents must comply with the Property Misdescriptions Act. Some of those who are supposed to know have said that the disclosure provisions of the Estate Agents Act and its subsidiary orders and regulations also apply to commercial agency. There is some logic in this. After all, the buyers and tenants of commercial space are consumers, too; they are just as deserving of protection as residential buyers and sellers.

During the mid-1980s, commercial agency enjoyed something of a bonanza. Although there is clear evidence of fee-cutting in the highly competitive climate of the recession, a commercial agent normally charges up to ten per cent of the agreed first year's rental. If the agent lets a single shop in a provincial parade for, say, £40,000 per annum, he will receive £4,000 for his pains. If he lets 30,000 square feet of

City of London space at, say £45 per square foot, he will receive £135,000. It is a matter of some argument as to which letting is the more difficult. It all depends on the market and the marketing; and depends on the economy – both local and national.

If an agent sold – as opposed to let – a building, it was customary to charge one per cent of the sale price. When some properties were sold to major financial institutions, either home-grown or strangely foreign, and carried a price tag of £50 million, one per cent produces a fee of a cool half a million. It has to be said that there are few transactions at this level and, when they happen, the shrewd vendor will have negotiated a more modest fee. But modesty is relative; after all, to wear a bikini in Cannes is virtually to be over-dressed. In the good times, commercial agents could let almost everything on which they took instructions. In consequence, staffs become inflated, but worse, the need for serious marketing know-how was low. When boom turned to bust, very few commercial agents – it's a young person's business – had the experience of coping with downturn.

Let us, for the moment confine our attention to the Property Misdescriptions Act of 1991. Commercial agents are, or were, just as fond of powerful adjectives as their residential colleagues; they are very fond of the word 'prestigious', for example. 'Landscaped grounds', as a phrase, slips lightly off the tongue, even if it means a straggly fir or two and an acre of grass which add mightily to maintenance costs. Car parking, if the numbers of spaces are not quoted, might mean a tight corner which keeps the re-spray boys in business.

There is an old adage about the three things which make for a successful commercial development: location, location and location. The commercial agents, therefore, spend much prose composition time on the question of location. The fact that the M25 is a mere two miles away is writ in bold letters, although access to the M25 may be a little troublesome on market day; and we all know what it's like when you reach the M25 in the rush hour when it's raining. These are sins of omission rather than description.

Some years ago, I was asked by an eminent London commercial agent to have a look at an industrial estate near Canterbury. From the brochure, the estate looked attractive. The buildings were well designed in both the visual and functional senses. The quoted rents were competitive. All main services were connected and there was adequate turning space on-site for even the most grotesque container lorry. But the agents couldn't shift it despite the fact that it 'afforded access to the motorway network'.

I drove down to have a look at it, not really understanding why, in a reasonably buoyant market, the estate was not letting. I recognised the buildings in the distance as I drove towards the site so the brochure was, at least, honest in one respect. I was within spitting distance of the estate when the level crossing gates clanked shut. A passenger train from one or other of the channel ports eventually turned up. It was longer than the platform. Having disgorged its passengers and taken on a few more, it then edged nervously forward until the driver was sure that his passengers in the end compartment of the last coach didn't have a four foot drop onto those nasty looking chippings. I don't know how many of you have jumped from even a stationary train, but it's nothing like landing on a gym mat. The whole performance took twenty-two minutes by an utterly reliable watch. Instead of driving on to the industrial estate immediately as I should – the developer expected me twenty minutes ago – I felt a compulsion to interview the station master.

It transpired that this happened eight times a day, both ways. And then there were the goods trains which didn't actually stop, but their passing through meant that the crossing gates had to be closed. Couldn't the platform be extended? Couldn't the passengers be told that, if they wanted to get off at that particular station, they should use the front three coaches? Well, that wasn't up to him, was it now? That was somebody else's problem. How many freight trains were there every day? Well now, that's hard to say. It just depends on the demand, you see. Yes, I understand that but, roughly, how many on a busy day? Oh well, it could be six or eight. I see – but the freight trains sort of rush through and the gates are closed only briefly? Ah, well, it depends if we're short-handed. I see – and where does the road beyond the crossing actually go? Go? Yes, go – I mean, where's the next town? Well, it doesn't go anywhere really so far as I know – never actually been up there.

Back in the car, I did some quick sums and calculated that, even in my most generous mood, the estate was cut off from the rest of the commercial world for about four hours in the average eight-hour working day. Lorry drivers could, if they wished, go for a drive in the country, but they would have to come back to the crossing sooner or later. I met the developer, who was sincerely proud of his buildings and, after apologising for my lateness, explained why. Yes, it was a bit of a problem, wasn't it? I felt it was rather more than a bit of a problem. Lord Beeching had long since left British Rail and the chances of closing the station seemed minimal. Mind you, said the developer, I bought the land at a giveaway price. Well, you could have fooled me. The brochure about this industrial estate was written long before the Property Misdescriptions Act, yet the draftsman had trod carefully. 'Afforded access to the motorway network' was the phrase. It was a bit like saying that there is access from Moscow to Nepal, but you have to climb K2 to get there.

The thinking behind the Property Misdescriptions Act is simply that the public must be protected against false or misleading description. Take shopping centres: when commercial agents are marketing shopping centres, they work out the millions of hungry shoppers within one, five and ten miles, expressed in distance and driving time. This is known as the shopping catchment. It has been said before that, if all the claimed UK catchments were added together, the country would have a population of about 200 million when all we have is a mere 56 million or so. The initial marketing of the centre is directed towards the retailers, particularly the big name multiples which create shopper-pull. If there is a less gullible crowd than the big multiple retailers, I have yet to meet it. They know more about shopping catchments than most agents, and adjectives leave them absolutely cold. Are these the folk that the Act is designed to protect?

People who buy or lease commercial space are in business – entrepreneurial minds which control companies and the lives of others. They are not usually very gullible either and I have yet to meet a buyer or lessee who committed himself to space without seeing it first, poking it and picking at the new paint-work with a nail file to make sure that there are two undercoats and a top coat. Is the legislation designed to protect them, too? It can be argued that, if a brochure or some detailed particulars of sale don't mention the adjacent gas works or the nearby tannery, the smell from which is pushed by the prevailing winds through the office windows, or the noise from the saw mill, it is misdescribing the property. Is it? There was a residential estate agent, anxious to sell a house in a poor market, who painstakingly air-brushed out of the photograph a large and very adjacent gasholder, but he has paid the penalty for that remarkable piece of enterprise. Notice, please, the word 'gasholder'; since I was old enough to know, they had been gasometers – but, no, gasometers they are not. They are gasholders. If, through ignorance, I describe them as gasometers in my innocent brochure, am I guilty of misdescription?

Bad though all of this may seem to be in respect of the Property Misdescriptions Act's application to commercial agency, it worsens dramatically if the other 'residential' requirements are applied to commercial agency too. Commercial agents are usually many other things as well. They can be economic planners; they advise on the form of development to suit their opinion of the market when a building is due for completion. They act as proponents in the rating war on one side or the other; they are valuers; they act as investment counsellors to pension funds of all sizes; they carry out rent reviews acting on both sides of the fence. They manage buildings in multiple occupation, shopping centres, industrial estates and business parks. Imagine, if you will, the kind of confusion which would arise if the 'residential' rules were applied to them.

A budding developer consults an agent on the form his development should take. A scheme is drawn up and the planning permission is granted. There is a fee for that. The agent can then project manage the job. There is a fee for that, and rightly so, because project management can be an absolute nightmare. The agent can also arrange funding; there is a fee for that – but, wait a minute, the funding might have come from a syndicate of the pension funds by whom the agent is retained. There is a fee for that; does the agent run to the developer and say 'Look, another department in my office has arranged funding for this job. I have to tell you so that you can decide whether you can trust me any more?' When the job is finished, the agent lets it; there is a fee for that. His investment department then sells the whole lot to the Japanese at a thumping profit, the pension funds take their profit and the developer takes his. Who does the agent tell about all these transactions in which he has been involved from the word go? The Japanese are just as likely to ask the agent to manage the completed development anyway – and, of course, there is a fee for that too.

Although everyone in the commercial example has been satisfied, it is possible that the developer could have achieved a better deal on initial funding than from his agent's pension funds. It is possible that the developer could have received a better offer than from the Japanese buyer his agent produced. The commercial agent may not be tied, in the sense that a residential agent owned by a building society or insurance company is tied, but the effect is very much the same.

All of this is not written to suggest that all of the estate agency regulations should be applied to commercial agents. It is written to suggest to the Government that the residential estate agent has taken something of a caning, which is largely undeserved.

13 THE FUTURE

There is no crystal ball. Nevertheless, a pattern of change has been established: dire threats hang over estate agents – both residential and commercial – and, of course, over the purveyors

of financial services. If the spate of Acts and Orders which now surround the business of property transfer is ignored by more than the expected handful who read nothing except the football results, worse will come. But, whatever happens, estate agents will still be with us, simply because the process of property transfer requires an efficient intermediary between buyer and seller.

The debate about estate agency has been going on for a long time. The debate will continue and there is a risk that pressure will grow for additional controls, agreed levels of competence (probably by examination) and stiffer penalties for the frankly naughty. The pressure will come not only from government and the Office of Fair Trading or, indeed, the general public; it will also come from the professional bodies representing estate agents – who have a poor view of everyone outside their particular clubs.

It is not too bold to suggest that estate agency will be with us for the foreseeable future and a bit beyond that. There was a time when local authorities were actively encouraged to establish residential agency departments; some of them did. It is not difficult to understand the logic of that particular departure into madness; at the time, local authorities were prolific lenders of money to house buyers. It seemed only a short step to provide total service. Local bureaucracies were, and still are, streets apart from the typical local estate agency – and you will remember that we have placed some emphasis on the unsocial hours, the energy and the caring. One or two – no, there were more than that, but precise figures are hard to come by – local authorities dipped large, gouty and expensive toes into the agency business. Some claimed success, but not for long. The point is made only to underline the fact that many attempts have been made to create a serious alternative to the present system. The attempts have been made because, as we have learned, the business of estate agency has been made to look too easy. If the debate has done nothing else, it has confirmed that estate agency is not easy – certainly, the experience of the Prudential and others in the big institutional brigade has confirmed that the business can be hard.

There is likely to be a reduction in the number of agency outlets, if only because the requirements of all those Acts and

Orders make the business more of a hassle than it ever was. The additional cost of administration – again because of those Acts and Orders, estimated to be over £300 per week for the average office – will reduce profitability. An alternative might be an increase in the cost of agency service; this is unlikely to appeal to those hundreds of thousands of vendors who think that they pay too much already. On the other hand, the European Parliament, in its quest for harmonisation, may demand standard rates throughout the Community. If that happened, there could be a surge of new agencies in the UK, simply because the UK fees would lurch upwards to match the French. If they didn't and the French fees lurched downwards to match ours, French estate agents would no doubt picket the cross-channel ferries and Heaven help the holders of passports which gave their profession as 'estate agent'. What the French do to sheep, they can quite easily do to estate agents.

There are some streets in the country in which every second shop appears to be an estate agency. On the face of it, there seem to be just too many estate agents, particularly when the residential market is near rock-bottom. There are two factors to consider on this question of numbers: if half the agencies are owned by the big battalions which are in the business primarily to offer financial services, they will not need to be all that profitable to survive. The riches they will attract through their financial services activity could justify their presence in prime locations. In any event, the big battalions have all learned lessons from the agency downfall of the mighty Pru and, as the residential market improves (as it will, for good cyclical reasons), the application of the principles of good, caring, local agency will ensure profitability anyway.

Quite apart from that, the concept of one-stop shopping – the combination of agency, financial services, surveys and conveyancing – will continue to appeal to practitioners whatever their specialisation. As public understanding increases of the range of services available under one roof, the trend is likely to be set. The trauma of house transfer will still be great enough for most buyers and sellers to want to take the easiest course. Comparison shopping for the best deal – and all the consumer protection bodies urge us always to compare – is not likely to appeal to house buyers to any great extent. It's all much too complicated.

The competition among the one-stop shopping emporia will increase. They will all seek both prime pitches for their outlets and representation in every town in the country. They will probably expand by acquisition rather than attempt to establish the outlets themselves. It is probable, therefore, that young, even the not so young, entrepreneurial spirits will establish new agencies, build them up quickly and sell them on. In fact, the development of estate agencies for sale could be the new way to become capital rich very quickly.

The independent agencies, whatever their size, could increasingly become 'tied' to particular financial services organisations, such as building societies and insurance companies. The 'free choice' which the cause of consumer protection so vehemently upholds may diminish. Buyers and sellers may not care about 'free choice', so long as they get what they want when they want it. Nevertheless, the fact that agencies will still receive 'multiple' instructions may create even more confusion in the already confused public mind. Each of the three or four agents offering the same property may easily be pushing quite different and distinct financial products. None of this will prevent the wily buyer from shopping around for the best financial package – but he or she will need an honours degree in financial management to understand the process. The fact is that there will remain some independent agency spirits determined to remain free of bondage to any particular financial house. If they get their marketing right and they have an adequate range of financial contacts, they could be favoured as estate agents by a discriminating public. But, for the public to be discriminating, they really do have to understand the process – which, for the moment anyway, is far too complicated.

It is the process of house transfer itself which demands change and, indeed, where the greatest change could arise. The professional bodies, including the powerful Law Society, are trying hard to help the government to get to grips with the problem. The start of change could be extraordinarily simple. Vendors could be required to produce an independent structural survey. It is a matter of fact that not every buyer bothers to commission a structural survey. The careful do and they may, if they are unlucky, have to pay for a survey on more than one house. When the residential market is buoyant and when the banks and societies are lending liberally, this is when gazumping is rife – and a buyer may be disappointed once, twice, even three times before he succeeds in a purchase. If he commissions a survey for each failure – and some do – the buyer could be many hundreds of pounds down. The structural surveyors should not complain. Many thousands of houses are now bought without surveys and, although the system would preclude the second and third surveys by the unlucky buyers, probably many more surveys would be required than is currently the case. In fact, the shortage of building surveyors might be a problem initially.

Proposals are already afoot to remove restrictive covenants after a stated period where they are no longer relevant. Those which should stick – for example, a ban on using a ground floor flat in a residential block as a fried fish shop – would, of course, remain. If the number of restrictive covenants could be dramatically reduced in this way, the Land Registry could record them and disclose them at the time of search. The Land Registry will eventually be totally computerised and efficient and will be comprehensive. Until that happens, vendors could equally be required to instruct their solicitors to carry out Land Registry and Local Land Charge searches, when their houses are offered for sale. This, as a start, would improve the pace of transfer and remove some of the risks that the present time-scale of transfer actually creates. If a house remains unsold for a long time, there is a chance that fresh searches will have to be made, but in ordinary market conditions the problem would not be a large one. In a buoyant market, which may be just around the corner, there should not be a problem at all.

Local authorities responsible for local land charges registers and responding to requisitions for official search might be persuaded to speed up the process, if the fees were increased to an economic level. The amount of work involved is considerable and the fees have never properly reflected the work loadings. Councils still have a major influence on our lives and the houses and flats we occupy, much more than may be apparent. It is, therefore, difficult to find an alternative system of responding to that awful list of supplementary enquiries which, you will remember, involved almost all departments of the authority. However, modern computer technology being what it is, there seems no reason, except money, why HM Land Registry couldn't centralise all registrable charges. Local authorities would be required to feed the Registry with everything, but that is probably too much to ask until after Armageddon. The immediate solution is to get the task moving as soon as a property is placed on the market.

There is some pressure to introduce the system of Scottish law which binds buyer and seller in a fairly tight knot very early in the proceedings. Much of the waste in the house transfer game is related to the risks arising simply from the passing of time – changes of mind, changes in circumstances. And, of course, it is primarily the passing of time which creates the opportunity for the dreaded gazumping in a buoyant market.

Great minds are now being applied to the simplification of the house transfer process. The simplification will undoubtedly come – so long as the legislators can sort out the vested interests from the honest impediment to change. Government has the power to force change and to finance it because, after all, change will need money. But we are talking about a market of many billions of pounds every year, a market in which a high percentage of us are shareholders and an even higher percentage want to be.

Whatever happens, the estate agent will still be there. His shop windows will still show those indistinct photographs; his detailed particulars of sale will occasionally raise an eyebrow in the Office of Fair Trading, anxious to ensure no contravention of the Property (Misdescription) Act, 1991. But he – yes, or she – will still be there. If he is good, he will be caring – doing his level best for his client, the vendor, and even more for his applicants. He will be worrying still about his vulnerable chains of sales and purchases, that damned roller-skate on the stairs, the lecherous dog and whether he has remembered to inform his client vendor about his hidden commission from the furniture remover.

Or she, of course!

INDEX

Also published by Mercury Books:

Alan Bailey

HOW TO BE A
PROPERTY DEVELOPER

Completely Revised and Updated

Foreword by Sir Christopher Benson,
Chairman, MEPC plc

'The developer's bible.' *London Property News*

'As well as being essential reading for the aspiring property developer and others in the property world, existing property developers should find it both useful and entertaining.'
Chartered Surveyors Weekly

'Worth a place on every property person's bookshelf . . . and a happy gift for all property friends. Fast and furious reading and sacred cows are butchered on virtually every page.'
Property Journal

'A warning as to the dangers as well as the opportunities and excitement of property development.' *Building Design*

ISBN 1 85251 115 X (hardback)   £14.95 net